# THE
# SPARK
## IN THE
# STONE

# THE SPARK IN THE STONE

### Skills and Projects from the Native American Tradition

## PETER GOODCHILD

Chicago Review Press

**Library of Congress Cataloging-in-Publication Data**

Goodchild, Peter.
    The spark in the stone : skills and projects from the Native
American tradition / Peter Goodchild.
        p.    cm.
    Includes bibliographical references.
    Summary: Introduces the highly successful wilderness technol-
ogy possessed by Indians of North America in the millenia before
white settlement. Includes projects for making simple tools,
weaving, and crafting moccasins and willow baskets.
    ISBN 1-55652-102-2 : $14.95
    1. Indian craft—Juvenile literature.    2. Indians of North Amer-
ica—Industries—Juvenile literature.    [1. Indian craft.    2. Hand-
icraft.]    I.Title.
TT22.G66    1991
745.5—dc20
                                                              90-27324
                                                                 CIP
                                                                  AC

Published by Chicago Review Press, Incorporated

ISBN 1-55652-102-2

    5 4 3 2

Manufactured in the United States of America

# CONTENTS

# ILLUSTRATIONS

*Beauty before me, I walk with.*
*Beauty behind me, I walk with.*
*Beauty above me, I walk with.*
*Beauty below me, I walk with.*
*Beauty all around me, I walk with.*

**Navaho Night Chant**

# INTRODUCTION

The Indians lived very successfully on the North American continent for at least ten thousand years—perhaps more than forty thousand years—without many of the things that white people now consider necessary for life: they had almost no metal tools, they raised no animals for food, and a great many tribes didn't even grow any plant food. The Indians lived by taking what they needed from their natural surroundings. They knew that almost every fish or animal could be caught to provide a meal, and thousands of different kinds of plants could be harvested for food or medicine. The carcass of a deer or buffalo could also provide hides for clothing, footwear, or shelter, the bones supplied tools, and from the sinew one could make rope. Stone provided knives, arrowheads, axe heads, hammerheads, drill bits. Flint also made sparks for a fire. The Indians were never lost in the woods, at least not in the sense that most white people can be, because Indians were at home wherever they were. They knew that the natural world could supply all one's needs—at least as long as one showed respect for that world and lived in harmony with the spirits of the wilderness.

When I talk about these skills, I will often be talking in the past tense, because I am mainly describing these arts as they were practiced before white people came to this continent. Most Indian techniques have been modified since those days.

When an Indian today goes hunting in the woods for food, he carries a modern rifle, rather than a wooden bow and flint-tipped arrows, although he may be using tracking skills that were developed thousands of years ago. However, some arts, such as basketry, pottery, and leather work, have changed very little since early times.

The Indians have a great deal to be proud of. They contributed far more to modern life than most people realize. In Ontario, for example, where I live, if I drive out into the country, what crops do I see being grown? Mostly corn, beans, and squash—all crops that were first grown by the Indians and that they taught the white settlers to grow. What else do I see? Sunflowers—again, an Indian crop. Other foods I might eat—although not all are grown in Ontario— include potatoes, tomatoes, peanuts, cassava, sweet potatoes, chili peppers, and cocoa; these are gifts of the Indians further south. Moccasins, toboggans, canoes, kayaks, teepees, snowshoes, parkas—all these things were invented by the native peoples of North America or their Siberian ancestors. By two thousand years ago, the Maya had the most accurate calendar that had ever been invented, and it remained the most accurate until recent times. Many medicinal plants that remain in use today were discovered by the Indians. Some of these drugs are South American in origin, but others are North American, including cherry bark, pine oil, witch hazel, and pennyroyal. Other herbs appear in both Indian medicine and in the herb books of medieval Europe. Did the two groups of people discover these plants independently, or did some long-ago cave-dweller teach the ancestors of both peoples?

What we shall be looking at in this book are some of those ancient secrets, those ways of living in harmony with nature and in close contact with nature. We need to know these skills. We gain strength from contact with the natural world. To grow up healthy, we need physical contact with a human mother, and to remain healthy we need physical contact with Mother Earth.

Have respect for the wilderness. If you see plants

of an endangered species, such as certain lilies or orchids, study them, but don't pick them. Don't kill an adult tree just for the sake of a small piece of bark. Use the whole tree if you are going to use it at all. (The Ojibwa Indians, for example, would use a birch tree for firewood after they had removed the bark from it.) Don't kill trees in parks and conservation areas, and don't touch trees on private lands without permission. Respect animal life. The Indians said prayers to the spirits of animals they had killed; they asked the spirits for forgiveness, explaining that the killing was from necessity, not from greed or bloodlust. Don't use Indian fishing or hunting devices if they are not permitted by the laws of your community, but learn how to make these things, nevertheless, because the knowledge might one day save your life.

# MAKING TOOLS

**A**lmost anything we make requires tools, but first we have to make those tools: we need knives, hammers, drills, and axes; a carpentry shop that will enable us to make some of the finer things in life. The Indians used a variety of materials: stone, bone, antler, horn, teeth, wood. Metal nails and screws weren't available to fasten parts together, so rope and glue of various sorts took their place.

## Stone Tools

Some kinds of stone are ideal for creating tools with a cutting edge, such as knives and axes. Other kinds of stone are not so useful in this respect, and only provide a dull edge. How do we distinguish between these kinds of stone?

For the point of view of the toolmaker, there are two general types of rock: smooth and rough. But you can't get a good idea of whether a rock is smooth-textured or rough-textured just by looking at the outside of it. The outside of a rock has been exposed to the weather for countless years or centuries, and all those years of sun and rain and frost will have changed the original texture of the rock. If you want to really see what type of rock you're dealing with, you have to break it in half and look at a clean, fresh surface. If we take a piece of granite, which is a very coarse type of rock, and smash it to get a fresh surface, and then look at that surface under a magnifying glass, we see that the stone is composed of individual speckles, or crystals—not very regular crystals, but crystals all the same. Granite has three kinds of crystals: clear, white (or pink), and black: the clear crystals are quartz, the white or pink ones are feldspar, and the black is either mica or hornblende.

If we look at a piece of sandstone, on the other hand, all we see are clear crystals, because sandstone only contains one kind of crystal: quartz, held together by a glue of some other kind of mineral, such as calcium.

If we break open a rock that reveals a smoother surface, we won't be able to see anything under an ordinary magnifying glass; the crystals are too small. Basalt is like that. Basalt is a very common grayish stone, often used for railroad beds, for example. It has a rather chalky or gritty feeling to it, so we couldn't exactly call it a smooth-textured rock, but it is certainly more fine-grained than granite or sandstone.

It's easy to confuse basalt with limestone or dolomite, two kinds of rock that are composed largely of calcium. Scrape the rock with a knife until you've got a little pile of powder. Put a drop of vinegar on the powder and look closely. If you see some foaming and bubbling, the rock is limestone or dolomite, not basalt.

Some kinds of stone are very smooth-textured. Look at a piece of broken glass, for example. The surface feels very smooth, almost slippery. As we turn it, the surface reflects light. Sunlight reflected off a piece of glass is quite dazzling; sunlight reflected off a piece of granite, on the other hand, would barely be noticeable. Ordinary glass is man-made, of course, but there is a kind of naturally occurring black or brown glass, called obsidian.

An appreciation of the different degrees of texture is important if we wish to understand how the Indians used these materials. Take another look at a piece of broken glass, preferably a thick piece, perhaps from the bottom of a soft-drink bottle. Besides having a smooth and shiny surface, thick glass is also interesting because of the way it breaks.

Some of the fractures will be rather unremarkable, but a lot of them will bear a peculiar resemblance to the inside of a clamshell. These are called conchoidal fractures, from a Greek word meaning "shell." When these clamshell fractures meet, the result is a sharp edge—perhaps a rather wavy edge, but a sharp one nevertheless. It was these conchoidal fractures that enabled the Indians to turn certain kinds of stones into efficient cutting tools. Coarser stones don't break with a conchoidal fracture. Granite, for example, just breaks into irregular lumps.

So now let's try making some primitive stone tools. These simplest tools were made by the Indians, but they were also made by a great many other "stone-age" societies. The people who built the great stone circle of Stonehenge in England thousands of years ago made flint tools that looked very similar to those used by the Indians.

Let's start by making the kind of tool that was used by early peoples all over the world. Scientists generally refer to it as a chopping tool. It was actually a general-purpose device, used not only as a chopper, but as a knife, an axe, a scraper, a wedge—for generally bashing other things into shape, in other words. Making such a tool only takes a few seconds, once you've got a suitable piece of stone. What you need to find is a nice oval stone, perhaps about as wide and as long as your hand, and fairly flat. The perfect place to look would be on a rocky shore of the ocean or of a lake, but you could also look along a riverbank, or on a mountainside, or wherever you can find a nice assortment of well-rounded pebbles. More important than the overall shape of this pebble is the texture of the rock that it is made of. You need to find a pebble made of a very smooth kind of stone, a texture closer to glass than to granite. You might find a reasonably fine-textured piece of basalt, for example, that gray stone I mentioned earlier. Some basalt is actually quite fine-grained, so that a newly fractured surface is quite glossy, almost waxy in appearance. More often, basalt is rather dull and chalky in texture, but even that kind of basalt might work.

1-1
**conchoidal fracture**

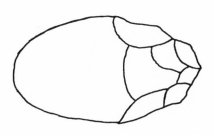

1-2
**chopping tool**

Another quite smooth stone you are likely to find is pure quartz, easy to recognize because it is usually snow-white and stands out clearly from other kinds of stone. Sometimes pure quartz breaks with a good cutting edge, sometimes it doesn't.

A common kind of golden-brown rock that is very good for toolmaking is quartzite, a sandstone that has been reheated underneath the earth so that it has formed a much harder kind of stone. The newly exposed surface of either sandstone or quartzite looks very much like sandpaper, but if you rub your hand over the surface of the stone, you can tell the difference between the two. Sandstone not only looks like sandpaper, it also feels like sandpaper, and the sandy particles might even rub off quite easily. The newly fractured surface of a piece of quartzite, on the other hand, feels a lot smoother than sandstone, and it might even have a fairly glossy surface.

But don't worry too much about the names of these different types of rock. Just find a kind of stone that breaks with a clean, smooth surface, not with a crumbly irregular surface. Find a nice oval pebble, about the size of your hand and fairly flat. Hold it in one hand, with one flat side up. Then take a another hard rock—which is called a hammer stone—and give your future chopping tool a fairly hard blow straight down near the tip. You should have managed to knock off a flake, which is more or less circular, from the underside of your chopper. Turn your chopper over, so that the fractured surface is now upward instead of downward. Strike the tip again, knocking off another flake just like the first. Knock off a few more flakes, if necessary, until you get the right shape. The end of your chopper should now have a sharp edge, somewhat like the cutting edge on a modern axe.

If it doesn't work, try another kind of stone. Finding the right kind of stone doesn't require a knowledge of geology, it just requires experimentation. When you find stones that seem to work better than others, take a good look at them. Memorize the appearance of that stone, so you'll be able to spot it again later.

When you've made a good chopping tool, you've created a duplicate of the gadget that all our distant ancestors used every day of their lives. A good chopping tool can be used to chop down a tree, especially if the base of the tree has been well charred by fire beforehand. The same tool could be used to put a point on a stick so that it could be used as a spear (and the spear tip would then be hardened by being held over a fire). Or the chopper could be used to skin an animal and carve up the carcass.

If you want a nice little "pocketknife," look at those flakes you knocked off in the process of making your chopping tool. Those flakes may not have the weight and bulk required for chopping down a tree, but they might have a much finer cutting edge than the chopping tool itself. Some Indians in the nineteenth century were still using flakes of that sort as tools. If the flake isn't quite the right shape, strike the edge with a small hard stone to break off small chips. You can even strike off a series of chips all along the edge to create a sort of saw-toothed finish that may be more useful than a straight edge.

Perhaps you're lucky enough to live in an area where you can find obsidian or flint. Obsidian, as I said, looks like dark glass. Flint is a bit harder to describe. (What we call flint is really chert, but we'll stick to the more familiar name.) Flint breaks somewhat like obsidian, although with not quite as much of a conchoidal fracture. It can be practically any color, but when you break it to get a fresh surface, it's quite smooth. The texture of good flint might be described as waxy or glossy—perhaps not glassy, but close to it. You might also say it looks a lot like hard plastic, although of course it's heavier than plastic. Good flint actually has almost a greasy look to it.

With obsidian and flint, the possibilities are endless, because the conchoidal fracture of flint and obsidian creates a very sharp edge. You might want to try creating a spearhead or an arrowhead. Spearheads and arrowheads are usually a lot harder to make than chopping tools or flake knives, but with flint or obsidian the task is not too difficult.

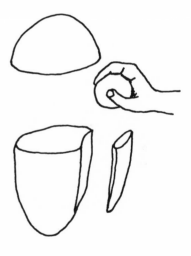

**1-3**
**chipping flint**

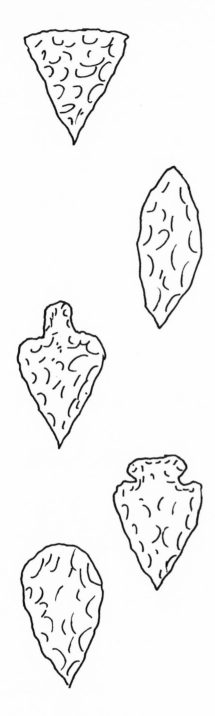

**1-4
arrowheads**

Try to find a large oval stone of flint or obsidian, perhaps about the size of a melon. Place it on a log or a stump. Find another round stone for your hammer stone, one that will fit in your hand, but preferably one that is harder than the flint or obsidian.

Strike a good-sized chunk off the end of the larger stone, so that the stone is now flattened at that end. Then tilt the stone up, so that the flattened end is uppermost. Strike down firmly on the flattened area, but near the edge of the stone. You will find yourself breaking off flakes that run lengthwise along the surface of the stone. Ignore these first few flakes, since one side of them will be cortex, the lighter-colored skin that covers the outside of a flint or obsidian pebble. Keep moving around the stone, striking off flakes all around, as if you were peeling a carrot.

Once that first layer of flakes has been removed, strike off some more flakes. Don't be afraid to put a bit of muscle into the task; weak blows crumble the rock, and may make it so misshapen that it is useless for any further work. Try to strike off flakes that are thin, flat, and as long as possible. And try to get the flakes to break off in such a way that the outer side of the flake has one or (preferably) two ridges formed by the removal of two previous flakes: a ridged flake is both stronger and more workable than a flake that is flat on both sides.

You'll probably find yourself going through a fair pile of pebbles before you produce some really useful flakes, but you may also surprise yourself with how rapidly your skill develops.

Once you have a few good flakes, you can try refining them into arrowheads. Find a smaller hammer stone, perhaps a quartz pebble about the size of a golf ball. Hold the flake on the ball of your thumb, and press down on it with the fingertips of that same hand. With the hammer stone, strike the flat surface of the flint chip, so that smaller flakes come off all along the edge. The reason for keeping the flake on the palm of your hand, rather than putting it down on a rock or a stump, is that the soft surface of your hand will distribute the pressure more evenly, and your future arrowhead will be less likely to break in half from all the hammering it is receiving.

Try to chip the flake into an elongated form: like an oval, but pointed at both ends. This is what scientists call a willow-leaf form. There are other forms that arrowheads can take, but the willow-leaf form is fairly easy to make. One end becomes the front of the arrowhead, and the other end is inserted into the wooden shaft.

You might want to put an even nicer edge on your arrowhead by getting a sharp-pointed piece of bone or antler and pressing this upward firmly against the edge of the arrowhead, breaking off chips instead of smashing them off. This technique is called pressure flaking.

It isn't absolutely necessary to have flint or obsidian in order to make arrowheads. If basalt is very fine-grained, almost waxy, then that will also do the trick, but fine-grained basalt is pretty rare. Quartzite is far more common, and often makes a reasonable substitute for flint. White quartz tends to break in a rather unpredictable fashion, but if you smash a few quartz boulders you may find some useable flakes. Quartz and quartzite and basalt are quite tough materials, so you might have to place the flake on a log or stump in order to chip the flake into shape, instead of just holding it in your hand.

Don't be surprised if you find making arrowheads a lot harder than making a good chopping tool. Human beings had been making chopping tools for many thousands of years before anyone got around to making an arrowhead or a spearhead.

In chapter 11 we'll be talking about how to make the rest of the arrow.

**Slate** Quite often one can find a medium-gray rock that breaks into flat plates, like the pages of a book—in fact, the individual plates might be almost as thin as paper. This rather strange kind of rock is slate, a stone that white people sometimes use for making roofs on houses. The Eskimos and Indians of northern Canada, however, used it for making all sorts of tools. Slate is a marvelous material to work with, partly because very little practice is required in order to become an expert at using it. Slate was worked by a combination of chipping and grinding.

For example, to make a knife out of slate, simply smash a chunk until you get a slab that is about the right size and thickness. Then place the slab on a large rock, and use a hammer stone to chip the slab into the outline you require. This chipping process doesn't produce conchoidal flakes, it just crumbles the edge in a crude sort of way. To finish the job, you need a large coarse rock to use as a grindstone. A chunk of sandstone is ideal for the job, but granite would also work well; it might be a good idea to smash that chunk of rock in half, to get a less smooth surface to work on. Then place the piece of slate on the grindstone and work it down to the final shape you want.

The Eskimos and northern Indians also made arrowheads out of slate, using the same techniques that I just described for making a knife. Slate arrowheads can be crafted to perfection, with a little time and patience. If you want to put a little stem on the arrowhead, so that it will have an overall sort of Christmas-tree outline and fit into the shaft of the arrow more neatly, then grind the arrowhead down on a sharp corner of the grindstone, rather than on the flat surface. Finish the grinding by switching to a less coarse type of grindstone. And if your grindstones get coated with grit, a good washing will restore them.

**The Pecking Method** If you're feeling really ambitious, you could try making a stone axe head by what is called the pecking method. Take a large oval pebble of a fairly fine-grained rock such as basalt. Find yourself a hard hammer stone, somewhere between golf-ball and tennis-ball size. Tap near one end of the oval pebble with hard, glancing blows, letting the hammer stone bounce off the surface. Keep up a steady rhythm, about one beat a second, or even twice that fast. After a minute you'll notice that a fine white powder is starting to trickle off the larger stone—not a lot of powder, just a few grains at a time. If you keep this up for a long time, you can work that rounded end of the stone into a flat edge, a blade. But don't start this job unless you're prepared for many hours of work, perhaps many days. If you persevere, you can actually work it to a fine edge. Then turn the stone around and peck a groove all around the axe head, so that you can later fasten on the wooden handle. Finish off the axe head by grinding it on one or two slabs of sandstone, or some other coarse-grained rock, and finish it off by grinding it on a smoother rock.

The handle is made from a freshly cut branch or a small trunk, about an inch thick and about two feet long. You'll need flexible wood for this; yew would be perfect, but willow or ash or oak would be quite good. Don't use wood from any tree with needles rather than leaves—yew is the one great exception to that rule—because needle-bearing trees are too brittle. Take the bark off and trim a foot of the handle to a thin strip. Plunge the wood into boiling water for a few minutes (or more), take it out, slowly bend the thin part tightly into a crook shape, and leave it like that until it dries. When it is dry, soak it in water again, preferably in hot water, bend it around the stone, with the wood gripping the groove in the stone, and fasten the whole thing tightly with a strip of slightly dampened rawhide several feet long.

## Bone and Shell Tools

Since it was not always possible to find the right kinds of stone for making tools, the Indians often used bone as a substitute. In fact, for making some kinds of tools, bone is a much better choice of materials than stone. For example, the cutting blade of a hoe was sometimes made by chipping a long piece of flint to the right shape and then fastening it to a wooden handle, but hoe blades were also made from the shoulder blades of large animals.

A small leg bone, broken and ground to a sharp point, was used as an awl, which was a tool for punching holes in animal hides when sewing clothes and moccasins. After the hole was punched, thread made of sinew was pushed through the hole. The best bone for making an awl is the ulna, a slender

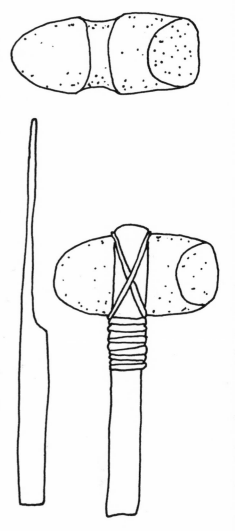

1-5
pecked-stone axe

bone about six inches long, in the front legs of large animals; just snap off the narrower end and grind the rest of the bone to a point.

The Eskimos, however, made real needles out of bone. They scratched two parallel lines, close together, on the surface of a flat piece of bone, and then pried that central sliver away from the rest of the bone. The sliver was ground smoother, and a hole was drilled in one end. This same technique of scratching deep lines—which is called incising—was used to make other kinds of tools as well; it was a slow technique, but it was more accurate than simply smashing a bone and hoping that one of the broken pieces might be the right shape.

Knives were made by cutting away (incising) one side of a leg bone so that it formed a blade; the joint at one end was left on as a handle. A similar kind of tool, a sort of draw knife or side scraper, was used for scraping the flesh and hair away from hides; it was made by cutting away one side of a leg bone, in the same way that knives were made, but leaving both ends on the bone, not just one.

Bone is an excellent material for making arrowheads, and for that purpose smashing the bone is probably as effective as incising, and certainly a lot faster. A rib bone from a large animal is ideal; whether it's raw or cooked doesn't really make much difference. Put one edge of the rib on a large anvil stone and hit the other edge a few times with a smaller stone. The rib will soon split in half. Smash each half into smaller pieces, and you will find that a lot of these pieces have a willow-leaf shape that makes them ideal for arrowheads. They just need to have their edges ground to a sharp finish. If you want to create a stemmed arrowhead, you'll have to grind two notches into the base, just as I described above for making stemmed arrowheads out of slate.

Another type of bone arrowhead was simply a sharpened tube-shaped section of a small bone, perhaps a leg bone from a small animal. One end was ground to a point, and the shaft of the arrow was pushed into the back of the tube.

Shellfish are another source of material for some

kinds of tools. The Nootka whale hunters on the coast of British Columbia used to make the blades for their harpoons out of mussel shells. Most shells would be far too weak for such a task, but what they used were the shells of a creature called the California blue mussel. The shell is about six or eight inches long and about a quarter of an inch thick. Other Indians used small kinds of shells for arrowheads, simply by chipping and grinding the shells into shape. Spoons were made out of clam shells by chipping and grinding one end of the shell to form a little stem that could be inserted into the split end of a twig; it isn't especially easy to do, since the shell is brittle and the stem part is likely to snap off if you go too fast.

## Woodworking

Indians didn't have saws, nails, or screws, but they still had ways of forming wood into various shapes and holding it together. To chop down a tree in the days before steel axes were available, an Indian would first plaster a thick ring of mud around the tree, about two or three feet above the ground. (If he couldn't find any good mud, he'd tie wet branches around the tree and keep them doused with water.) Then he would build a fire all around at the base of the tree. As the fire burned, it would start to burn away the base of the tree; the mud would prevent the rest of the tree from catching fire. As the wood below the mud started to turn black, it was chopped away with a stone axe.

If an Indian needed a flat piece of wood—a strip or board—he would take a narrow log from which he had removed the bark, stand it on end with its narrowest end uppermost, and hammer wedges into it until the log split in half. The wedges were made of hard wood, of antler or bone, or even of stone, and usually several wedges were used on a single piece of wood. The first wedge had to go through the center of the log, however; if he were to insert the wedge off to one side, away from the center, then after he hammered the wedge, the log wouldn't split in half evenly; the split would run off to one side, leaving him with two rather misshapen and useless pieces. After the first wedge had been hammered in, other wedges were inserted beside the first one, or along the side of the log, or wherever they were needed. The log was now in two pieces. Another split in one of these pieces produced a reasonably flat board.

The Eskimos sometimes cut deep grooves along the side of a log before inserting the wedges, to make sure that the wood would split in the direction they wanted it to.

Wood was also bent into shape, to make parts for snowshoes or canoes, for example, by leaving it to soak in water for a few hours or days, weighted down by a rock. The task could be speeded up by soaking the wood in boiling water, or by pouring boiling water over it. Sometimes a pit was dug in the ground, a fire was built in the pit, and rocks were heated in the fire until they were very hot. The burning firewood was removed. The piece of wood to be bent was placed in the pit on top of some vegetation, and dirt was thrown in to finish covering the pit. Water was then poured onto the dirt and allowed to seep down to the hot rocks, where it would turn to steam and soften the wood.

Wood was usually fastened with rope of some sort, as we shall see. The Eskimos used a sort of nails when they were making their kayaks. They drilled holes in the wood, then hammered in pointed rods of wood or antler, which we call treenails. The treenails had to be very dry, because wet wood or antler would have shrunk later on, and then fallen out of the holes.

Glue wasn't used very often, although pine pitch was sometimes put into the forward end of an arrow shaft to hold the arrowhead in place, or glue could be made by boiling small bits of hide or antler tips for many hours until it melted. The Eskimos sometimes used heated blood as a glue in their kayaks.

One rather humble but important wooden tool was the digging stick, used to get edible roots out of the ground, to make holes for planting crops, and for getting clams and other kinds of shellfish from the beach. To make a good digging stick, take a three-foot log of a hard wood such as oak or ash, about three or four inches thick, peel the bark off, split the wood into quarters, and then trim one of those quarters into a rounded shape with a point at the bottom. It's true that any old stick could be used as a digging stick, but the advantage of making one out of wood that has been quartered is that you are avoiding the pith, the innermost part of the tree, which is too soft to hold a point.

# 2

# ANIMAL FOOD

Almost any creature in the animal kingdom can provide food, but it might be best to start by explaining what kinds of animal food are *not* safe to eat. Up in the Arctic, the Eskimos tended to avoid the livers of polar bears and certain kinds of seals, because these animals had so much vitamin A in their livers that people would have become sick from eating it. On the West Coast, the mussels, oysters, and clams are often dangerous in the summertime because of a poisonous organism that gets into them: watch out for signs posted on beaches and other places. The Indians actually ate a lot of insects, especially in the Southwest, but there were a few kinds that had to be avoided, mostly butterflies, moths, and adult beetles; the usual rule was that if it tasted bitter, it probably wasn't very digestible.

But insects are high in protein and certainly worth considering as food. The most popular insect dish was grasshoppers. Catching grasshoppers was mainly a community affair; people would dig a pit near the grasshoppers, several feet deep, and then make a big circle around the pit and the insects. They would then walk inward toward the pit, hitting the ground with branches, forcing the grasshoppers to jump into the pit, from which they would be scooped up to be boiled or roasted. Roasted grasshoppers were sometimes later crushed into a powder to be used in soup. Grasshoppers aren't bad tasting; they're a bit like unsalted peanuts.

Other sources of animal food were the many kinds of shellfish. Not only were two-shelled creatures such as mussels, oysters, and clams eaten (except on the West Coast during the summer), but also the one-shelled beasts: the periwinkles and whelks and other kinds of snails. The two-shelled kind are called bivalves. The one-shelled kind are called univalves. Clams are a kind of bivalve, and there are several kinds of clams. They are generally found below the surface of mud or sand, somewhere between the high-tide area (the top of the beach) and the low-tide area (the edge of the sand at low tide), and each kind of clam has its own preferred place to live. Some kinds prefer to burrow near the high-tide zone, other prefer the low-tide zone. Some kinds prefer to live in mud, others prefer sand. The easiest way to spot clams is to watch for their squirts as you walk near them. When you see them spurting water in this way, dig a hole beside some of these spurts, and then start digging sideways toward the clams to get at them.

Another important source of animal food was fish. Most Indians ate fish to some extent, although the Plains Indians ate very little. Some of the Indians of northern Canada lived mainly on fish, and so did some of the Eskimos. Fish are a terrific source of protein, even though most of the freshwater varieties don't provide enough fat for a steady diet.

The Indians had many ways of catching fish: sometimes they used a hook and line, somewhat as we do today for sport fishing. Other methods are more like the techniques used by commercial fishermen today, involving nets of various sorts. But the Indians also used traps, spears, harpoons, and bows and arrows, and sometimes they even caught fish in slow-moving water by adding substances to the water that would poison or stun the fish without making their flesh poisonous for humans.

Hooks were made of wood, bone, antler, shell, or even stone. Some were made of one piece of material, some were made of two. One-piece bone hooks were

**2-1**
**one-piece hook**

made by taking a large flat piece of bone and scratching the curved design of the hook on it. By deepening these scratches, the hook could finally be lifted away from the rest of the bone. The hook was sanded to shape, and a little groove was cut around the top of the shank to hold the line.

The two-piece kind of hook is easier to make. There are several variations, but basically it involves tying a pointed bit of bone or hard wood—a thorn would also work—to a wooden shaft. The top of the shaft is carved to form a knob to hold the line, or a groove is cut around the shaft. Tie the string to the shaft, and weave it back and forth around the shaft and the point in a series of figure eights about a dozen times. If you make the hook entirely out of wood, you'll have to tie a small piece of stone or bone to the top of the shaft, to get it to sink.

Another simple device used for catching fish was the gorge. Sharpen a sliver of bone at both ends, and carve a groove around the middle, or drill a hole through it, to hold the string. When the fish swallows the gorge, it turns sideward and catches.

The hook or gorge was fastened to a string, which in turn was fastened to the end of a pole. Hooks and gorges were often baited with meat, dead fish, or insects. At other times, a lure would be used; it was usually dangled from the end of a separate line.

A very common kind of fish trap was the weir, basically a fence or wall built across a river. Often the weir was V-shaped, with the point of the V usually downstream, so that the force of the current would carry the fish down into the trap. The point was kept open wide enough for the fish to swim through into some sort of corral. The Eskimos made the trap (straight, not V-shaped) out of boulders placed across a shallow river, while further south the trap was usually made of poles planted in the riverbed.

2-2
two-piece hook

2-3
stone weir

**2-4
log weir**

An improvement on this setup was to place a basket trap at the point of the V. Basket traps were made in all sizes, from about three feet to over twenty feet long. To make one, the Indians arranged a couple of dozen long thin poles in a cone shape and fastened hoops inside or outside them to keep them rigid. They fastened a shorter cone inside the mouth of the first one. The trap was tied to the point of the V, and a few heavy rocks were placed inside to hold the basket trap down on the bottom.

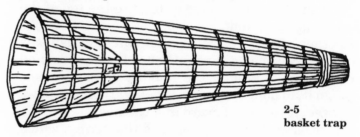

**2-5
basket trap**

Nets took many forms, from long-handled dip nets to much larger seine nets that were drawn around whole schools of fish, but perhaps the most common was the gill net, so called because its mesh was large enough for a fish to put its head through, but small enough that the fish would get caught by the gills. You could make one out of the cords of a parachute, for example, if you were ever in an airplane and had to make an emergency landing in the middle of the wilderness.

A gill net is really nothing more than a long series of girth hitches. You'll need many yards of string, and you'll also need a gauge for measuring the squares of the net, and a shuttle to hold the string as you weave. The gauge is simply a rectangular piece of wood about four inches wide. The shuttle is a flat piece of wood about six inches long and about two inches wide, with a deep notch at each end; the string is wound onto the shuttle and then unwrapped as you go along. In an emergency, you can get by without either a gauge or a shuttle, just using your left hand as a gauge and keeping the string wound up in a ball instead of on a shuttle, but it isn't as easy to keep things tidy that way. You'll also need a length of heavier cord, which you'll later run all around the net.

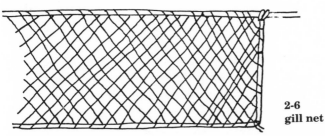

2-6
gill net

Plant two poles firmly in the ground, or fasten them to two trees, about as far apart as the length that you want your net to be, perhaps twenty feet. Tie the string to top of the right-hand pole, maybe four or five feet off the ground. Let out enough string to reach to the left-hand pole, bring the string back around the pole, and then tie a girth-hitch knot loosely around the top length of string, about four inches along. Insert the gauge into the big loop that you're tying off; pull the knot tightly up against the gauge. Let out a little more string as you move to the right and make another knot in the top string. And so on. When you've worked your way all the way back to the right-hand pole, take another turn around the pole and do another row of loops and girth-hitches underneath the first row, going in the opposite direction.

Keep going back and forth, with each row under the previous one, until you reach the ground. Keep everything tight, and you'll have a nice regular net. The knots slide, so you can always adjust them a bit afterward, but you can't really adjust the overall size of each square. It's important to keep the string pulled up tight against the gauge each time, before you tighten the knot.

When you've finished the bottommost row, run the heavier cord through each of the topmost loops, then

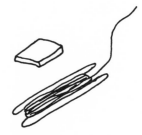

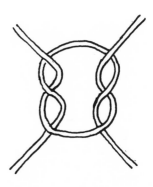

2-7
girth hitch

down through all of the loops on one side, along and through the bottom loops, and then up the second side, where its two ends can be tied together. This cord will protect the net from strains that might otherwise damage it. Remove the poles, and the net is complete. When you want to put it in the water, though, you'll need to tie pieces of wood or bark along the top edge, and small rocks along the bottom edge, so that the top of the net floats and the bottom of the net sinks.

There were various ways of setting a gill net. If a creek was narrow enough, it might be possible to fasten the net right across from one bank to another. If not, then one end was tied to a tree or stake on the shore, and the far end could be pulled out into the water by someone swimming or in a canoe, and fastened to a long pole planted in the riverbed, or the end could be kept in place by a big float at the top and a big anchor stone under the water. One good place to put a gill net is where a river has little whirlpools; fish often rest and feed in these spots.

Reptiles and amphibians never formed a large part of the Indian diet, but sometimes lizards were clubbed or speared for food. Snake is certainly a worthwhile emergency food; there isn't a great deal on a snake fillet, but it tastes quite all right. In the southeastern United States, turtles were sometimes caught with a piece of meat fastened to one end of a line, with the other end of the line tied to a pole stuck in the riverbank. I don't know if frogs were eaten by the Indians, but they're an excellent source of food. Bullfrogs can easily be speared from a canoe (split a stick partway, to make a two-pronged spear); peel the skin off the legs and fry them, with butter and garlic if possible.

Grouse and other birds were caught in snares, which might be set up in a circle around some grain thrown down as bait. Ducks and geese were most easily shot or corraled during the summer molting season, when they were unable to fly. The Eskimos sometimes used a bola to bring down birds from a passing flock. The bola was simply three rocks encased in leather pouches, which in turn were attached to cords joined together at the end. The cords were whirled around the head and let loose at the right moment.

Mammals were caught in traps, which can be roughly divided into two types: deadfalls and snares. A deadfall is a log or rock held by a support attached to some sort of trigger mechanism; when the trigger is moved, the support falls, and the log or rock lands on the animal. Usually some sort of bait was attached to the trigger in order to attract the animal. Snares, on the other hand, sometimes had triggers and bait, but they didn't always have, since the trapper often just set the snare in the animal's regular path, hoping that the snare would be invisible to the animal.

Snowshoe hares, muskrats, and beavers were often trapped or shot by northern Indians, although the inhabitants of the north also killed caribou, seals, walruses, whales, and bears. Porcupines could be easily clubbed, and hence formed a good source of food in emergencies. Further south, deer and moose were common big-game animals, while sheep, elk, and antelope were taken in other areas. The Plains Indians, of course, lived largely on buffalo; in the early days they drove the buffalo over cliffs or into long fence-like traps with corrals built at the bottoms of steep slopes (a lot like the V-shaped fish traps—but, of course, much larger), but when horses became available, the buffalo were just rounded up and shot. In parts of the southwestern United States, smaller animals, including mice and pack rats, provided a large part of the diet. Rabbits were killed with throwing sticks, sometimes after they had been driven into long nets by community drives—long lines of people walking toward the rabbits, driving them toward the nets.

Game should be bled and gutted soon after killing. The Indians used blood to make soup, and the liver, kidneys, and most other organs were eaten right away, since they can't be preserved easily. About the only organ that isn't edible is the gall bladder (although deer don't have one), next to the liver. If you eat woodchuck, porcupine, opossum, or raccoon,

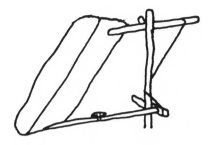

2-8
deadfall

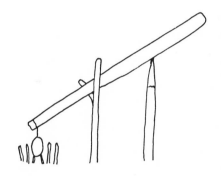

2-9
snare

it is best to remove the kernel-like glands in the flesh, which can affect the flavor of the meat; there are two in the small of the back, and one on the inside of each of the front legs. Muskrats have glands in the front legs and a corresponding set in the back legs. Wild game is also improved by parboiling it before further cooking, or by covering it for a day or two with cold water to which about half a cup of vinegar has been added.

The Indians preserved fish by splitting them in half and hanging them up to dry in the sun, although often a smoky fire was built underneath. The flesh of larger fish might be slashed a few times to speed up the drying. Very small fish sometimes weren't split or gutted, but just strung up and smoked.

The meat of mammals was preserved in very much the same way. In the drier and warmer parts of North America, the meat was cut into strips and hung over poles to dry in the sun, but in other areas a small fire was kept lit under the meat; the fire didn't heat the meat or even smoke it very much, it just kept it dry. The meat was usually dried for several days, until it was somewhat leathery in texture, then packed away until it was needed, at which time it would be softened by boiling.

# 3

# PLANTS FOR FOOD AND MEDICINE

There were many hundreds of plants used by the Indians for food. The ones described below are just the most important ones. There are many others that I haven't listed, for various reasons: generally because they're too rare to be of much use, or because they're too much bother for the small amount of food you can get out of them.

Where there's any chance of confusing one kind of plant with another, I've also given the scientific names. Common names have the bad habit of being applied to several different plants. If you really want to be able to recognize wild plants, you should try learning these scientific names.

## Cultivated Plants

In what is now the eastern United States, in the Southwest, and in a few other areas, Indians grew most of their food. The main crop was Indian corn, which we also call maize. Modern kinds of corn, which give us popcorn, cornmeal, corn on the cob, and so on, are all descended from Indian varieties of corn. Beans and squash were also important crops, grown in the same parts of the continent as corn. Sunflowers were grown in many areas, but mostly in the Southwest.

Try growing an Indian garden one summer. Corn,

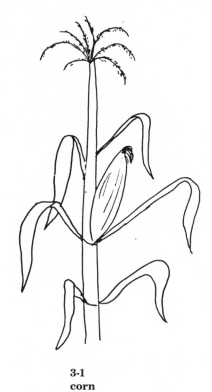

**3-1
corn**

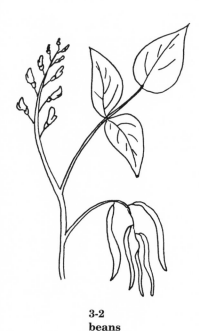

**3-2
beans**

beans, and squash all need to be planted late in the spring, when all danger of frost is past, but that didn't stop the Indians from growing these crops quite far north; even the Huron Indians of southern Canada had large corn fields.

Corn needs fairly rich soil, and it takes up a lot of room, since the full-grown plants have to be grown quite far apart. It also needs a lot of light, so don't plant it where trees or houses are going to cast a shadow. Usually the Indians put several kernels in each hole, assuming that animals and birds would eat some of the corn before it had a chance to grow.

When the corn began to ripen, some of it was picked to be eaten as corn on the cob: the husk was left on, and the ears were shoved into the ashes of a fire, or they were pit-baked (see chapter 4). Most of the corn was left on the plants until it had dried, and the ears were then picked and hung up to dry more completely indoors. The dried kernels were later crushed into a powder, either by being pounded with a huge wooden mortar and pestle, or by being crushed between two stones, the bottom one wide and flat, the top one smaller and rounder. The finished cornmeal was used to make several kinds of soups, pudding, or bread.

Like corn, beans were planted several to a hole, so that even if some didn't sprout, or if they got eaten by animals, enough plants would grow tall enough that the animals would leave them alone. Several kinds of beans were grown, and the Indians planted the beans in the same rows in which the corn was planted, with the vines of the beans running up the stalks of the corn. That way more food could be grown on a piece of land than if the two crops were planted separately. When the beans began to grow, some of them were eaten in the pods, in other words as what we call green beans, but most of the crop was allowed to completely ripen on the vine until the beans were fully grown and had become hard and dry. The pods were then pulled from the vines, and the beans were stripped out of the pods and stored until they were needed. Usually the dried beans were either roasted or boiled.

Squash was enjoyed by Indians in many parts of the continent, and there were several kinds grown, including pumpkins, which are really just a large species of squash. Squash takes a long time to grow, and some of the Indians around the Great Lakes planted the squash seeds indoors and let them grow inside until the weather was warm enough for the seedlings to be moved out into the garden. When the squash was fully grown, it was peeled and then cut into strips or spirals and hung up to dry. Not much of the plant was left unused: long before the squash fruit itself is ready to pick, the flowers fall off the plant, and these flowers were saved and added to soup. And when the squash fruit itself was harvested, the seeds weren't thrown away; instead they were roasted lightly and eaten like peanuts.

You might want to try preparing a squash in the Indian style. With a sharp knife, peel the outer rind off and cut the squash in half. Scoop out the seeds and separate them from the fibers. Cut the squash into slices about half an inch thick, poke a hole through each slice, and run a string through them all. Hang the slices up for a day or two, and they will shrink quite a lot and become wrinkled and dry. When they're completely dry, you can store them in a jar for as long as you like. When you want to cook some of the squash, let it soak overnight in a pot of water, and the next day put the pot on the stove and boil the squash until it is cooked. But while the squash is still drying, you could put the seeds in a pan and leave them in a hot oven for a short while, until they turn a slightly darker color. Take them out and they're ready to eat.

Sometimes sunflowers were grown in a garden, but other Indians just found them growing wild. The seeds have an excellent flavor, and they are rich in oil and therefore quite filling. Try planting a few sunflower seeds in a sunny patch of garden and watching them grow: by the time they've finished growing, they'll look more like trees than flowers. Let the dinner-plate-sized flowering heads go to seed, and then cut them off and bring them indoors to finish drying. But a word of warning: sunflower

3-3
squash

seeds also win first prize for popularity among birds and squirrels, so be prepared for some competition when the seeds start to ripen.

There is one kind of sunflower that wasn't grown for its seeds, but rather for its underground tubers, and that is the sunflower called Jerusalem artichoke—although it isn't an artichoke and it doesn't come from Jerusalem. Like most sunflowers, Jerusalem artichokes grow to well over the height of a man, but the flowering heads are a lot smaller than those of the sunflowers we usually see. The tubers of the "artichoke" grow just under the ground, or even sticking up a little bit above the ground. They look like rather knobbly potatoes; some of them will be tiny, others can be the size of your fist. But they grow very well, usually producing an abundant harvest, even in poor soil. They like to be growing in a sunny spot, but they don't really need much care in order to produce lots of tubers, which should be dug up after the first frosts. To grow them, all you do is plant a few of the tubers several inches deep, keep them watered, and let nature take care of the rest. They aren't at all hard to grow; if anything, they'll take over your garden. The only catch is trying to find a few of the tubers to get you started with your garden, since a lot of gardening centers don't carry them. Try a few large supermarkets, or perhaps a health-food store.

Jerusalem artichokes taste somewhat like new potatoes, but much nicer, with a faint additional flavor somewhat like sunflower seeds—as we might expect. Jerusalem artichokes are quite nice raw, but you can also cook them. Don't bother peeling them. If you want the best flavor you should be sure they're freshly picked, and then only cook them for a few minutes, just enough to soften them slightly. They are a highly underrated vegetable, and well worth considering if you want to try growing your own food.

## Wild Fruit

The Indians ate many kinds of wild berries and other sorts of fruit. White people are familiar with a few kinds, but often miss other types that are equally abundant and just as nice in flavor.

Blueberries we probably all recognize, since they grow in most parts of North America. There are several species, but they all grow as shrubs, from one foot to several feet tall, and the leaves are small, pointed, and an attractive glossy green. The flowers are tiny and bell-shaped, white, pale pink, or pale green, with five little teeth on the rim of the bell. The berries are at first pink, and then red, and then a deep dark blue. They are ready to pick in the late spring or early summer. Some Indians gathered great quantities of blueberries, and for many tribes of eastern Canada they were the most important of all plant foods, especially in areas that were too far north for food to be grown in gardens. They weren't picked one by one, the way white people pick them; instead the Indians used their fingers as a rake to gather the berries into a blanket. Indians in other areas beat the bushes with a stick, letting the berries fall onto a hide or blanket.

When the berries were harvested, the leaves and twigs were picked out, and the berries were spread out on mats to dry in the sun. Blueberries only needed to be left outside for a day if it was hot and sunny, but if they took longer they were taken in overnight, so that dew wouldn't fall on them and wet them again. The dried berries were kept in baskets and saved to be eaten all through the winter.

The next time you collect some blueberries, try spreading them out on trays in the sunshine and letting them dry. If you want to dry a lot of them, you could try using an old sheet, except that whatever you use is going to get stained from the juice. A sheet of plastic is also a possibility, but don't lay the plastic out on your front lawn, or the sun's rays will turn the plastic into a miniature greenhouse and burn the grass underneath. Move the berries around once in a while, so that they dry all over. The blueberries will eventually shrink and become hard and dark, looking and tasting a bit like raisins. Put them in an old jar, and you can store them just like that for as long as you like.

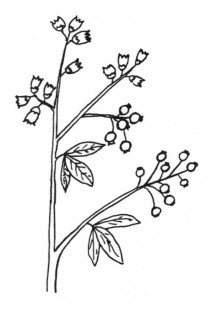

3-4
blueberries

In the United States, Indians gathered huckleberries, which are very similar to blueberries except that they stay red when they are ripe.

Almost any other kind of fruit that the Indians picked was preserved for later use by drying it in the same way that blueberries were dried.

Another very popular kind of fruit was the raspberry, which is also well known to white people. There are many kinds of raspberries, and a lot of them don't go by that name. All raspberries grow on thorny bushes. Each berry is a soft mass of tiny balls, and the center of the fruit is somewhat hollow, but the color can vary from pink to black. One of the most common kinds is the black raspberry, or bramble, that grows in vacant lots, along dirt roads, and along railroad tracks, spreading its great looping vines covered with sharp thorns. Other kinds of raspberries are called dewberries, salmonberries, cloudberries, bake-apple berries, and so on.

One fruit that the Indians appreciated but that most white people don't know about is the one that gave its name to a city on the Canadian prairies. Saskatoon, shadberry, shadbush, shadblow, sugarberry, serviceberry, juneberry—I'm not sure if that completes the various names of the fruit (or the entire plant) in the English language alone, never mind the native names. There are several kinds of juneberries, and even botanists find it hard to tell them apart, but basically there are short shrubs, two or three feet tall, and then there are tree-sized juneberries. Juneberries are related to apples, and they have tough, fine-toothed dark green leaves that look a lot like apple leaves. The berries themselves— which, as the name indicates, usually appear in June—look like tiny red apples, about the size of peas or sometimes larger. They also taste a lot like apples. The ones on the small shrubs seem to have more flavor than the ones that grow on trees.

We're all familiar with strawberries, I'm sure. The fruit is red and hairy, growing just above the ground, and the leaves grow in threes, like clover, except that they have teeth. Wild strawberries are much smaller than cultivated ones, but the wild ones have so much

3-5
juneberries

more flavor. The only problem is that there are hardly ever enough to make a real harvest out of them.

Cherry trees grow in most parts of North America, though again the fruit is rarely collected by white people, perhaps because it is usually rather sour or bitter. Wait until the autumn before gathering them; one or two good frosts will make them sweeter tasting. The Indians discovered that the flavor of many kinds of fruits is improved by frost. Don't eat any other part of the cherry tree, since all these other parts contain cyanide, which is a poison. The Plains Indians used to gather large quantities of choke-cherries and lay them out in the sun to dry. They dried the cherries with the stones still inside, and then pounded them up, stones and all, before adding them to the dried-meat mixture called pemmican. But I would recommend that you spit out the stones; chokecherry stones may not be as poisonous as the stones of other kinds of cherries—black cherries are the worst—but it's better not to take the risk.

Wild grapes grow in most parts of the United States and southern Canada. The vines, climbing slowly with their corkscrew tendrils, often creep all the way up to the top of tall trees, and some years the harvest can be quite bountiful. As is true of most wild fruits, they are smaller but tastier than the culti-vated varieties. Don't mistake Virginia creeper for grapes. Grapevines have large heart-shaped leaves; Virginia creeper has five leaflets forming a palm shape.

Crowberries, small black fruit growing on tiny shrubs that look like miniature spruce trees, were eaten by the Eskimos and the northern Indians. Cranberries are another northern fruit, common in wetlands, but they also grow in many parts of the United States.

Salal berries, which look faintly like blueberries but which grow on bushes with tough oval leaves about two inches long, are quite common on the Northwest Coast. Oregon grapes are another fruit often eaten on the Northwest Coast. They aren't really grapes at all, but they look and taste like them,

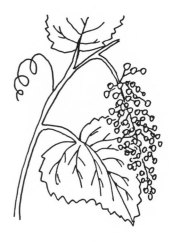

3-6
wild grapes

3-7
high-bush cranberries

**3-8
squawberries**

**3-9
May apple**

although the leaves are stiff and have large prickles like holly leaves.

High-bush cranberries aren't at all related to real cranberries. They are common in the northern United States and southern Canada. The bushes are about six or ten feet high, and the leaves have three pointed lobes, so they look a little like maple leaves. Even after a frost they are still rather bitter, and yet they were often eaten. White people sometimes make jelly out of the berries. The jelly has an odd sour taste that is at first unpleasant, but you may find, like me, that you begin to really like it.

Sumach berries were used in most parts of North America. The common species of the east is staghorn sumach (*Rhus typhina*), which has branches that look and feel like a deer's antlers "in velvet." The palm-like leaves give the shrub a strangely tropical look. The tightly packed cluster of dry, fuzzy red berries was crushed slightly and dropped into cold water to make a beverage that tastes like iced tea with lemon. The fruit of a sparser-looking species of sumach, called squawberry (*Rhus trilobata*), was used to make a beverage in the southwest.

In the eastern parts of the continent, Indians enjoyed eating the strange fruit of the May-apple plant, which also looks as if it belonged in some distant tropical country. The plant is only about a foot high but it has big leaves. The fruit grows in the center of the plant and looks somewhat like a smooth-skinned lemon. The flavor is also somewhat like that of a lemon, but perhaps more like that of a pineapple. You can eat the whole fruit, including the skin. Don't eat the rest of the plant, though.

In the southeastern United States, pawpaw trees produce a long brown fruit with a yellow pulp. In the same areas, persimmon trees produce red fruit the size of baseballs. The pulp is very soft, but it's delicious and filling.

In the Southwest, many kinds of cactus supplied fruit. Prickly pear has stems shaped like beaver tails, and the young stems were often eaten as well as the fruit. The fruit looks like a small red or green potato, and some kinds have prickles that need to be brushed off. Cut a thick slice off each end, and then cut a deep slit all along the prickly pear. You can then peel the thick leathery skin off, as easily as removing a glove. What's left is a pink oval that looks a lot like watermelon and even tastes like watermelon, but much nicer. The only catch to eating them is that they are full of hard black seeds. They're too hard to bite, and there are too many of them to be picked out. The answer is simple: you swallow them. They pass through your body and don't do any harm at all.

The fruit of the saguaro, a tall and stately cactus, was important in southern Arizona and nearby parts of Mexico. Wolf berries (*Lycium* spp.) grow on thorny bushes with toothless leaves. Manzanita berries (*Arctostaphylos* spp.) get their name from a Spanish word meaning "little apple," which is what they look like. The leaves are tough and evergreen, and the southwestern plants are related to a more northern plant called bearberry.

Yucca plants are easy to identify by their long stiff leaves, growing in a cluster like a bundle of swords. Two species, both called datil (*Yucca baccata* and *Yucca arizonica*), have banana-shaped fruit that was eaten raw or cooked (usually pit-baked all night). The flowers and the peeled stems of another kind, called palmilla (*Yucca elata*), were also eaten in the Southwest.

That by no means exhausts the kinds of fruit that the Indians harvested. I haven't discussed crab-apples, rosehips, hawthorns, gooseberries, currants, bunchberries, barberries, or elderberries, for example, mainly because there aren't usually enough of them to be worth picking, although they certainly aren't rare either. Go easy on raw elderberries; they aren't really poisonous, but some people get sick if they eat a lot of raw ones.

But above all: don't eat any fruit unless you know what kind it is. There aren't that many poisonous kinds of fruit, but if you start eating baneberries or nightshade berries, you could make yourself quite sick.

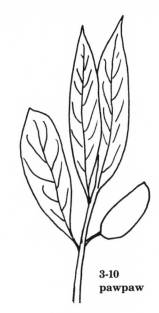

3-10
pawpaw

3-11
prickly pears

3-12
wolf berries

# Other Common Wild-Plant Foods

**Nuts** Indians gathered and ate the nuts of many kinds of trees: walnuts, butternuts, hickories, pecans. Chestnuts also used to be an important source of food, but about a hundred years ago a disease killed off most of our native chestnut trees. Hazelnuts were often picked while the nuts were still green. Nuts were eaten fresh, or they were made into soup, or they were stored for the winter. Quite often they were crushed and dropped into boiling water, so that the oil inside the nuts would float to the top of the water, where it could be scooped off and saved as a separate item of food.

**Acorns** were eaten in many parts of North America. There are several kinds of oak trees that acorns grow on, but there are basically two types, the white oaks and the black oaks. All oak leaves are divided into several large lobes, but the difference is that black oaks have pointed lobes, while the white oaks have rounded lobes. The acorns from white oaks usually taste better than the acorns from black oaks, but most kinds of acorns tend to be bitter. It's not that they're poisonous, it's just that they have a lot of tannin in them, which is the same stuff that you can taste if you leave a tea bag sitting in hot water for too long.

The Indians had all sorts of ways of soaking acorns to get the tannin out, and you might want to experiment a bit to find the best method. With white-oak acorns, one effective way is to crack them to get them out of their shells, then drop them into a fair amount of boiling water. Let the water boil for about ten minutes; it will turn brown. Get rid of the water and boil them again in some more water. Do this two or three times, and the water should stop turning brown. At that time the acorns can be drained again, and they're ready to eat. There might not be much taste at all by then, but they can be added to bread or soup to provide extra nourishment. The same method can be used with black-oak acorns, but it takes several hours of boiling. Another technique is to put the shelled acorns in a weighted basket in some shallow running water for several days.

**Cattails** (*Typha* spp.) A marvelous writer named Euell Gibbons called cattail "the supermarket of the swamps." The plant grows almost all over North America, but it was mainly eaten by the Indians of Utah and Nevada. The plant grows in marshes, either in several inches of water or at least in fairly soggy ground. It has tall narrow leaves, looking like some sort of enormous grass. Toward the middle of summer, you'll see a perfectly straight stalk growing up the center, and at the top of this stalk there is a vertical cigar-shaped thing which is made of the minute flowers of the cattail.

Several different parts of the plant are edible, and none of it is poisonous. First of all, if you dig up the entire plant you will notice that right at the bottom, there is a long horizontal "root" that looks like a withered old carrot or parsnip. It isn't exactly a root, it's a rootstock—an underground stem. You can pull up these rootstocks at any time of year, though autumn is probably the best time to collect them. If you wash one of them in clean water and break it open, you'll see that it is white and starchy inside, like the inside of a baked potato. But there are also lots of fibers running along through the starchy material. The Indians cooked these rootstocks by pit-roasting them or pit-steaming them, or sometimes they just held them over a fire for a few minutes to cook them. When they had cooked the rootstocks, the Indians chewed them for a few minutes, swallowed the starchy parts, and spat out the fiber. These rootstocks are pretty bland-tasting, but they're filling, and they could certainly keep you alive for a while. The fact that they are available all through the year—including winter, if you could get through the ice or frozen soil—makes them an important emergency food.

In the springtime, you can eat the shoots, the cluster of new leaves. It's best to gather them when they're about a foot or two high. Reach down into the water as far as the bottom of the stem, and then just snap it off from the rootstock. The shoot looks

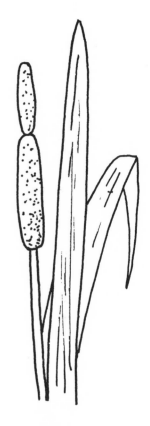

3-13
cattail

something like a leek plant, or a giant bamboo shoot. It's white at the bottom, and then gradually turns green further up the leaves. The part you eat is mainly the white part, since it's crisp and tender. The white part can be broken off with your hands, or you can use a knife. But don't throw the rest away yet: if you peel off one or two layers of leaves, you'll see the white part goes further up inside the shoot. So save this inside part as well. The white parts can be eaten raw, but they'll have a slightly marshy taste, and they're much better cooked. Put them in a pot with some water and boil them for a few minutes, and you have a pleasant-tasting vegetable. If you're cooking them at home, you can always add a little butter.

There are other parts of the cattail plant that the Indians ate. For example, when the shoots have grown taller, around the middle of summer, the central stalk produces its cigar-shaped top. The "cigar" is actually the flowering head of the cattail, though the flowers are so tiny that it is hard to recognize them as such. While the flowering heads are still green, but several inches long, they can be broken off and eaten like corn on the cob.

Even later in the year, the flowering heads turn brown. If you knock one of them, a fine yellow dust is likely to blow away from it. This dust is actually pollen, and it can be boiled to make a sort of hot cereal, or it can be made into bread, perhaps added to other kinds of flour. The tricky part is collecting enough of this pollen. You have to watch your cattail swamp pretty closely as the flowering heads turn from green to brown, and that means making a visit almost every day, waiting for the day when the pollen production is at its height. When the pollen comes off the cattails in great golden clouds, get a bag and go around dipping the heads into the bag to shake off the dust. If you've chosen the right day, you should be able to get enough to make yourself a bowl of bright yellow porridge.

**Bracken Fern Fiddleheads** The Indians ate several kinds of ferns. Sometimes they dug up and cooked the rootstocks, but they also ate the fiddleheads, which are the young fronds before they have begun to open in the springtime. These young fronds are called fiddleheads because their curly shape makes them look like the end of a violin. It is sometimes hard to tell one kind of fern from another, partly because ferns don't have flowers, which are usually the most distinct part of a plant. No fern fiddleheads are known to be poisonous, however, although some of them are too bitter to eat.

One type of fern that is easy to identify is bracken or brake (*Pteridium aquilinum*), because it always has three fronds coming from the central stalk. Most other ferns have only a single frond on each stalk. The young plant has three little fiddleheads together at the top of the stalk, whereas on other ferns each fiddlehead comes out of the ground individually.

**3-14
bracken fern**

Bracken fiddleheads are brittle, and so they can be snapped off from the base of the stalk quite easily. Boil the fiddleheads for only a couple of minutes, and they are ready to eat. It was mainly the western Indians, from Alaska to California, who enjoyed bracken fiddleheads, but the plants are also common in the east.

Don't eat bracken fern when it gets older. If animals eat a lot of fully grown bracken they get sick. Bracken at that stage is so tough that you aren't likely to want to eat it anyway, but I thought I should warn you in any case.

**Arrowheads** (*Sagittaria* spp.) Along the edges of lakes in much of North America, there is a plant that has big leaves shaped like arrowheads, and that is how it gets its name. Arrowheads usually grow in several inches of water. They don't grow more than about a foot high, so from the shore the leaves and flowers are all you can see. The flowers are quite pretty, a brilliant white, with five round petals. In the autumn, the arrowhead plant develops round tubers at the ends of its long thin roots. The tubers look a little like potatoes, and they also taste like potatoes, but much nicer.

Wait for a warm day in the autumn, because you have to get your feet wet, and lake water in autumn can be cold. Wade out into the lake, and stir up the mud with your hands or your feet, until you find some of these tubers. They grow only slightly below the surface of the mud, so they aren't hard to find. Don't look right next to any plant, because the tubers grow several feet away. When you've collected them and cleaned them, they only need to be boiled slightly to be eaten. Many Indians gathered these vegetables. The ones they didn't eat right away were boiled, sliced, and strung up to dry, to be eaten later in the year.

**Common Milkweed** (*Asclepias syriaca*) gets its name from the milky sap that oozes freely from the plant when it is broken. Common milkweed is a pale green all over, is rather downy or fuzzy in appearance, and has a fairly thick stalk and leaves. It is only found in eastern and central North America.

Three parts of the plant were eaten. In the spring, when the shoots come out of the ground and are only three or four inches high, cut them off and drop them into several inches of boiling water for five minutes (make sure the water is boiling *before* you put the shoots in), and you have a tasty vegetable that is a little like asparagus. When the plants get bigger, the flowers start to develop, and these form a ball-shaped cluster, with fifty or a hundred blossoms all growing from the same point. Collect these clusters of flower buds and cook them the same way you cooked the shoots. A few weeks later, the remaining flowers will have turned into the familiar fat knobbly seedpods. While these seedpods are only about an inch long, you can pick them and boil them the same way. The Indians sometimes ate milkweed raw, but I advise you not to, because raw milkweed is slightly poisonous. It doesn't taste very nice uncooked anyway.

Don't mistake milkweed for Indian hemp or dogbane, which are related and look slightly similar. Indian hemp and dogbane also have milky juice, but they have pretty pink bell-shaped flowers in much looser clusters. Milkweed flowers have a peculiar hourglass shape.

There are other kinds of milkweed than the common one, usually thinner and less of a dull green, but all with the hourglass-shaped flowers. The

Indians ate about eight different species of milk-weed, but some of them are a bit dangerous, so I don't recommend that you eat any of them but the common one described above.

**Dandelions** weren't growing in North America before the arrival of white people, but it would be a pity not to mention them. They have certainly been eaten by Indians in many areas of this continent since the plants became widespread. In the spring, before the flowers start to grow, take a knife and slice off each dandelion plant just at the top of the root, so that the whole crown of leaves stays together when you pick it up. Get rid of any leaves that are longer than a finger (more or less), because they'll be too bitter. Wash all your dandelion leaves and drop them into boiling water, and you have a fine-tasting vegetable.

**Onions** Wild onions (and garlic and leek) can be found almost all over North America. They look a little like some kinds of poisonous plants, but an easy way to tell if you dealing with an onion is to smell it, since they all smell pretty much like the kinds of onions you buy in a supermarket. Wild onions aren't very big, though; they look more like the kind we call green onions.

**Amaranth** (*Amaranthus* spp.) A plant that you'd be quite likely to find growing as a weed in a garden or in a farmer's field is a rather ordinary-looking thing with dark slightly yellowish-green leaves and a top that looks a little like a very tiny head of broccoli. The plant is called amaranth; it also has the less dignified name of pigweed, but that's confusing because the name "pigweed" is also applied to one or two other plants. Another name is "redroot," and the color of the root can help you to identify it. Amaranth was an important food plant to many Indians in North America and further south. The young leaves make a fine green vegetable, and the seeds were added to bread.

**Miner's Lettuce** (*Montia perfoliata*) is a small, pale, delicate-looking plant, and the leaves are often joined together so that the flower seems to be growing out of the center of a little cup. The plant was used in many parts of western North America. The plant was eaten raw or cooked, and often the whole plant was used, including the roots.

**Mountain Sorrel** (*Oxyria digyna*) is another plant found over most of the west. The leaves were gathered in the spring and eaten raw or cooked.

**Clover** (*Trifolium* spp.) There are many kinds or clover, both wild and cultivated, but they all have the three tiny round leaves and the equally tiny cluster of flowers (white, pink, or yellow), although some of the wild clovers grow into bushes several feet high. All clovers are edible, and the western Indians often ate the whole plant, from seeds to roots, raw or cooked.

**Dock** (*Rumex* spp.) The leaves of several kinds of dock were eaten in the east and the west. The kind called curly dock (*Rumex crispus*) is a common weed that grows in many gardens; it was brought to this continent (perhaps accidentally) by white settlers, but the Indians soon adopted it as a vegetable. In the Southwest there is a native kind of dock called canaigre (*Rumex hymenosepalus*); the leaves, stems, and seeds were eaten. Change the water once or twice if the taste is too bitter.

**Chenopodium** (*Chenopodium* spp.) You may know this plant by the name of lamb's quarters, since it is this species that is so often found as weeds in gardens all over North America. The leaves are diamond-shaped, and underneath they look as if they had been dusted with white powder. It's a European plant, not a native one, but it was adopted into the native diet; pick the young plants, or the tops of the older plants, and boil them very lightly for a nice green vegetable, or collect the small black seeds later on and use them for bread or porridge. All the chenopodiums are edible, but go easy with the seeds of Mexican tea (*Chenopodium album*), since they're a mild poison, which was mostly used for getting rid of intestinal worms.

**Cambium** In the springtime, all trees produce a clear paper-thin layer of material called cambium, right between the wood and the inner bark. Cambium is very wet and soft, a sort of clear film that can be scraped off with a dull knife and eaten raw, straight off the tree, once the bark has been stripped off. Sometimes the cambium has a rather strong flavor, especially if it comes from an evergreen tree, so you might want to spit out some of the juice when you're eating it. However, pine trees were the most common kinds of trees from which cambium was taken.

All evergreens supply good cambium, with the exception of yew, which is poisonous. Tree-sized yews only grow in the west, but there are shrub-sized ones in the east. Yew has flat needles about half an inch to an inch long, and the undersides of the needles are a slightly yellowish green (in fact, the tops also have a rather dark yellowish tinge, compared to other evergreens). Yews also have bright red fruits, but often there aren't any growing. Look at a good field guide, if you have any doubt about a particular kind of evergreen.

Other trees from which the Indians took cambium were birch, poplar, maple, alder, basswood, slippery elm, and red ash.

Having said all that, I should also say that it isn't a good idea to go about taking the bark off trees just for the sake of a few handfuls of cambium, because you could kill or injure the tree, and you will certainly disfigure it. If you want to try cambium, wait until someone is chopping a tree down for some other use. But it's important to know about cambium, because it's one of the most common kinds of plant food that would be available in an emergency.

**Waterlilies** (*Nuphar advena, Nuphar polysepalum, Nelumbo lutea*) were eaten in the east and the west. The big white or yellow flowers and the broad floating leaves can be seen on almost any woodland lake; just under the mud there grows a big, exotic-looking root, often three or four inches thick and several feet long, rather starchy or spongy inside. Collect the root either late in the fall or early in the spring if you want it to taste best, although it still has a rather bitter flavor, and you might want to change the water several times when you're boiling it. In the fall, the seeds can be roasted or fried. A type of waterlily called American lotus (*Nelumbo lutea*) has big yellow flowers and strange bowl-shaped leaves; it is found mainly in the more central parts of the United States, and it has good-tasting potato-like tubers and large edible seeds.

## Edible Wild Plants of Particular Regions

The plants described above can be found in most parts of the continent, or at least in a good half of it. But there were also edible wild plants that grew only in certain areas. To avoid having you waste your time looking for plants that just don't grow in your area, I will list the others by region.

**The Eastern Woodlands** Around the Great Lakes, and to some extent further south, the Indians gathered huge quantities of wild rice (*Zizania aquatica*), which grows along the shores of lakes. They went out in canoes and used sticks to knock the rice grains into the bottom of the canoe. When the canoe was full, they brought the rice back to shore, spread it out to dry, roasted it, and crushed it slightly to remove the chaff (the outer coating). Then the rice was tossed up into the air on a windy day, so that the wind blew the chaff away—although other Indians preferred to save the chaff and eat it.

In the southeastern United States, the roots of greenbriers or catbriers (*Smilax* spp.) were important foods. Greenbriers are usually thorny vines or small shrubs, with big heart-shaped leaves and a cluster of tiny dull green flowers; the berries, usually blue-black, grow in small clusters. Don't eat the berries, but the young shoots of the plant can be cooked and eaten as well as the roots.

Groundnuts (*Apios americana*) are vines that look like bean plants, to which they are related, but the part that was eaten was the underground tubers, about the size of a walnut. Cook them and eat them while they are still hot.

All the different sorts of maple trees were used for making syrup and sugar, both in the east and west of the continent, but mostly in the northeastern United

States and eastern Canada. In the early spring, an axe was used to make a large slanted cut in the tree. A small board was jammed into this cut, and the sap ran along the board and dripped into a birch-bark container on the ground. The sap was boiled down until most of the water was driven off, and the result was maple syrup. If this was very gently heated even further, and well stirred, the syrup crystallized into sugar.

**The Plains and the Plateau** Other kinds of food plants were found in the center of the continent, or up in the Plateau area—Oregon, Idaho, eastern Washington, and eastern British Columbia. Certain kinds of roots were especially important. Prairie turnip (*Psoralea esculenta*, and all other the kinds of *Psoralea*), which has several other common names, is a low-growing clover-like plant that was the main wild plant of the Plains Indians. Somewhat further west, the Indians gathered other roots: yampa (*Perideridia gaidneri*), biscuit-root (the various species of *Lomatium*), balsam-root (*Balsamorhiza* spp.), and bitterroot (*Lewisia rediviva*, which is now rare).

The bulbs of edible camas or wild hyacinth (*Camassia quamash* and *Camassia leichtlinii*), a kind of lily, were very important in the West. The edible camas usually has six blue petals, although they are sometimes white, while a very poisonous species called death camas (*Zygadenus nuttallii*) usually has green or greenish-white petals; don't touch any camas bulbs unless you're absolutely sure of what kind they are. The difference in the flowers may have made identification easier, but the bulbs of edible camas were usually dug up after the plant had gone to seed.

**The Southwest** Agave or mescal (*Agave palmerii* and *Agave parryi*) looks somewhat like yucca but has thicker, toothed leaves; some species have thin leaves, but these kinds were not used. Don't eat the raw plants, or they will burn your mouth. In the late spring or early summer, the Indians used to chop down the plants with a big wooden chisel, and cut off the tops of the leaves to expose the huge white crown, which was roasted in a pit for one or two days.

**3-15
prairie turnips**

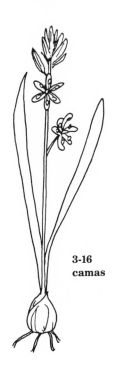

**3-16
camas**

Instead of using a pit, you can bake the crown, covered, in an oven, for ten hours at 350 degrees.

In northern Mexico and the nearby parts of the United States, two kinds of wild beans were important: mesquite (*Prosopis juliaflora*) and screwbean (*Prosopis pubescens*). On the salt flats of the southwestern United States, the leaves and seeds of the various species of atriplex or saltbush (*Atriplex* spp.) were eaten; the plant looks like chenopodium, to which it is related. Two green vegetables of the Southwest are beeweed (*Cleome serrulata*) and monkeyflower (*Mimulus* spp.)

An important food throughout much of the Southwest was the nuts of the various kinds of pine trees called pinyon pines; the nuts were roasted by tossing them in a basket with live coals. Then the shells were cracked, and the nuts and the broken shells were winnowed by tossing them up into the air on a windy day, so that the wind would carry off the shells.

The seeds of wild grasses were sometimes the most important wild-plant food in the Southwest, especially four species that had seeds that separated easily from the chaff: dropseed (*Sporobolus contractus*), giant dropseed (*Sporobolus giganteus*), alkali sacaton (*Sporobolus airodes*), and Indian millet or Indian ricegrass (*Oryzopsis hymenoides*). But many other kinds of grass seeds were eaten. The usual way to harvest them was to hold a basket under the seed heads and beat them with a stick.

## Wilderness Medicine

The Indians used hundreds of plants for curing illness. To treat fever, cold, coughs, rheumatism, or headaches, for example, they would pour boiling water over a handful of the inner bark of willow and let it steep for a few minutes before drinking it. The taste may be bitter, but willow bark actually contains a substance that is closely related to aspirin. Poplar bark was used for most of the same medical problems, and it has the same aspirin-like ingredient. The Indians of the Southwest often made a tea of mesquite leaves to treat headache, and the needles, bark, and resin of all the needle-bearing trees were made into a tea for treating colds—but as I said, avoid yew.

There are several kinds of plants called wintergreen, but the one the eastern Indians mainly used was a plant that is only an inch or two high, with hard, shiny, dark green leaves, and the scientific name of *Gaultheria procumbens*. The leaves are oval, almost round, with only a few tiny teeth, and when they are broken they give off a wonderful odor that is precisely the same as the wintergreen flavor we sometimes taste in candies. The name, however, comes from the fact that the leaves stay green all winter long. Sometimes you can find a few red berries on the plants; the berries are quite edible, and they have the same wintergreen flavor as the leaves. But to the Indians it was the leaves that were more important, since a tea made from the leaves was considered useful for treating headaches or rheumatism. In fact, like willow, the plant contains a substance related to aspirin.

Another plant that was used for mild headaches was mint, which was made into a pleasant-tasting tea. Mint tea actually tastes best if the plants are hung up to dry first for a few days. Mint tea was used not only for headaches, but also for treating colds, and for gas or other kinds of stomachache.

The Plains Indians preferred treating both colds and stomach problems by chewing the root of the calamus plant (*Acorus calamus*), or by making a tea out of the root. The plant itself, which grows on the edges of ponds, is rather odd-looking, with straight, tall leaves almost like an iris, but with a dull green flowering head poking out from halfway up the rather flattened stem: this flowering head looks more like a pine cone than a cluster of flowers. The root is fat and rubbery and has a slightly bitter but pleasant flavor, something like the taste of nutmeg or cloves. In any case, the Plains Indians thought calamus root, chewed or made into a tea, was good for almost any kind of medical problem, from toothache to snakebite—although I can't personally guarantee that it'll cure everything.

For treating diarrhea, many of the eastern Indians

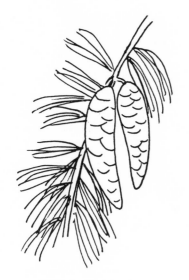

**3-17**
**eastern white pine**

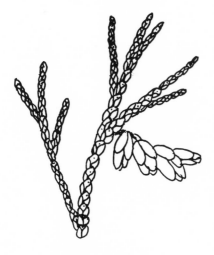

**3-18**
**eastern white cedar**

made a tea out of the inner bark of any of the various kinds of oak. For the opposite problem, a number of eastern tribes made a tea of dandelion roots as a mild laxative and a general tonic (an old medical term meaning "something that improves your overall health"). A lot of western tribes used the roots or leaves of all sorts of sagebrush as a treatment for stomachache.

On minor cuts, sores, and burns, many eastern Indians used the pitch of various evergreen trees: pine, cedar, spruce, hemlock, tamarack, or balsam fir. The mashed inner bark of these same trees was used for the same purpose. The easiest of these trees to get pitch out of, however, is balsam fir, because the tree has bubbles of blisters on its bark. If you pop one of these bubbles, a clear thin resin pours out.

Witch hazel (*Hamamelis virginiana*) is one of many medicinal plants discovered by the Indians. The Ojibwa Indians poured boiling water over the inner bark to make a lotion for any sort of skin problem. The Menominee Indians boiled the twigs as a lotion to rub on sore muscles.

The Indians had a number of ways of dealing with insect pests. They often put bear grease on their skin to keep away biting insects—in fact, they used any sort of animal oil, fish oil, or vegetable oil to prevent sunburn in the summer and frostbite in the winter. In the Southwest, the Indians used to rub wild onions on their skin to keep insects away, and if they got stung by insects they crushed the leaves of Rocky Mountain beeweed (*Cleome serrulata*) and placed them on the skin. The Rappahannock Indians of the eastern United States used dried pennyroyal leaves (*Hedeoma pulegioides*) to keep fleas away, while the Eastern Cree burned the dried leaves of Canada fleabane (*Erigeron canadensis*) for the same purpose. The Blackfeet used the crushed flowers of pineapple weed (*Matricaria matricarioides*) to get rid of insects. The western Indians scattered sagebrush leaves on the ground, or burned them, to keep insects away, and the Indians of the far north burned sphagnum moss, rock tripe (a kind of lichen), or anemone, to get rid of biting insects.

If you find yourself having some sort of medical problem some day when you are far from a doctor, you might consider trying one of these Indian remedies as a kind of first aid. None of the above remedies contains any poisonous substances if it's used in a reasonable dose. However, if you have a medical problem that won't go away, get to a doctor as soon as possible. There may be more to the problem than you think, and it's best to let a doctor decide what kind of treatment is needed.

**3-19
spruce**

# 4

# MAKING FIRE AND COOKING

There's an old saying that "home is where the heart is," but we could also say, "Home is where the hearth is." A little campfire in a circle of rocks can make you feel quite at home in the wilderness. On a cold autumn evening, that fire provides light in what otherwise might be a long dark night, and a hot cup of tea from water boiled on that fire is always pleasant. But there's more to it than that. Perhaps it's the wonderful smell of wood smoke, or the way we seem to drift off into strange imaginary worlds when we peer into the red caverns within the glowing coals. Whatever the reason, there's an undeniable magic in a campfire, and a pleasure in sitting by a campfire that can't quite be equaled by the central heating in our modern houses. I've never understood why people would pay such tremendous prices for houses that don't even have fireplaces. What's a winter night without a cheery fire?

I remember when I was trying to build a tiny log cabin on some land I'd bought in Ontario. I spent the first day cutting down trees and hauling them over to where I was going to build the cabin. Toward the end of the day I piled a few logs up into a sort of four-sided fence, even though they weren't peeled or notched yet. I sat on a rock and stared at the pile of logs, squinting at it, trying to imagine it as some sort of a home. It didn't work; it just looked like a pile of logs. Then I realized that night was rapidly approaching, and that I'd better get all my tinder and fuel together while it was still light enough to see, if I intended to have a fire that evening. When I got a good blaze going, I flopped down beside it, deciding that I wasn't going to do any more work that day. My fireplace wasn't much, just a circle of heavy rocks on a big patch of bare rock just south of where I was building the cabin. But for the first time that day, I really felt at home. I actually felt comfortable, I felt relaxed, I felt that I was where I belonged. My partly built log cabin couldn't give me that feeling, but a simple campfire could.

The discovery of how to make and control a fire was one of the greatest achievements in human history. Fire gave warmth and brightness during the long cold winter nights, and fire cooked people's meals. Fire made it possible for people to travel north into Siberia and work their way slowly— generation by generation—into Alaska and the rest of North America.

A fire is made of three parts: the *tinder*, the *kindling*, and the *main fuel*. The tinder is some sort of fine material that burns easily, such as shredded bark. The kindling is slightly heavier material, such as twigs. To start a fire, you place a small wad of tinder in the center of the fireplace, pile a little teepee of twigs over it, and light it. When the twigs are burning well, the main fuel goes on: the logs— dead wood, of course, but preferably not wood that's been lying on the ground. If you don't add enough wood to a fire, it will go out, but a fire will go out just as easily if you add too much wood too quickly. Make sure that the wood that is already on the fire is blazing well, before you add any more.

The Indian fireplace was usually quite simple, just a ring of heavy stones, or sometimes a mound of stones. The stones helped to keep in the heat of the fire, so that even in the morning there would be a few sparks still glowing. Whoever woke up first could drop a few bits of tinder on those sparks and blow gently until a new fire began to blaze.

Indian food was often boiled. Even meat was generally boiled, whereas white people are more likely to prepare meat by roasting it. Clay pots were used to boil food, and the pot was usually placed right on the ground, and a ring of fire built around it. Sometimes, however, the pot would be suspended by a rope around its neck.

A lot of Indians didn't have clay pots, either because they lived in areas where there was no clay, or because they moved around a lot and they didn't want to be carrying anything as heavy as a clay pot. So instead, they boiled food either in very tightly woven baskets or in containers made of sheets of birch bark. (On the Northwest Coast, Indians used wooden boxes. The Plains Indians just dug a shallow pit and lined it with a piece of rawhide.) These baskets weren't usually placed directly on the flames. Instead, rocks were heated in the fire. Wooden tongs were used to pick a hot stone out of the fire and drop it into the water and food in the basket. The rock might be rolled around a bit to prevent it from burning straight through the bottom of the basket. When that rock cooled, it would be lifted out and another one added. This method sounds rather primitive, but it really doesn't take long to get food to boil by this method. Don't use rocks that have been lying in water, because they might explode, and don't use sandstone, because it will crumble. Quartz (a very white rock) and flint are also said to be inclined to explode.

Indians did roast meat fairly often, though, by sticking it on a wooden spit and holding it over the flames. They also baked meat, by wrapping it in large leaves, such as corn husks or skunk-cabbage leaves, and burying it in the ashes of a good hard-wood fire that had burned long enough to be mostly coals and ashes rather than bright flames.

A favorite method of cooking, especially in western North America, was pit cooking. A pit was dug in the ground, perhaps one to three feet deep. A fire was built and lit at the bottom of the pit, and large stones were placed on the fire to heat. When the stones were red hot, the coals and any remaining unburned wood were removed from the pit, or at least pushed around until the flames had died down. The food was placed on top of the stones, perhaps after being wrapped in leaves. Everything was covered with some sort of vegetation, such as bark or grass, and soil was piled over the top of this. The pit was left for a few hours. The temperature of the rocks was always slowly going down, so there was little chance of the food being burned. Some kinds of food were left for days in these pits. Since the making of these pits involved a certain amount of work, this kind of cooking tended to be a community affair.

A variation of pit cooking was pit steaming. The pit was dug in the usual way, the rocks were heated by a fire, and the food was added, but wet seaweed was piled on top of the food before the whole thing was covered with soil. The rocks heated the seaweed and created a lot of steam, and it was the steam that cooked the food. This technique is imitated by white people nowadays in seaside clambakes.

There was another way of pit steaming. Again, the pit was dug, and the rocks were heated in a fire, and the food was added. But while the dirt was being put in, a stick was placed so that it stood straight up in the middle of the mound. When all the dirt had been put on, the stick was carefully pulled out, so that there was a hole leading down toward the food. Water was poured down this hole, and as it hit the rocks down below, it created steam.

The Indians used to start a new fire from the sparks of an older fire, or from a neighbor's fire. When they were traveling, they would carry a piece of cedar-bark or sagebrush-bark rope (or sometimes just a wad of the bark, hidden in a clam shell or a buffalo horn). This rope would be lit before they went on the trip, and if it was watched carefully it would stay lit throughout the journey, so that it could be used to start a fire when camp was finally made. It wasn't kept burning as a flame, but only smouldering, like a cigarette. But there were times when no spark was available, and it was necessary to create a new one.

## Making Fire with Stones

Sometimes a spark was created by bashing two stones together: two pieces of pyrite (a copper-colored type of iron ore), or a piece of pyrite and a piece of flint or quartz. Sometimes two pieces of flint or quartz were used, without the pyrite, but making sparks that way is not so easy. Later on, the Indians adopted the white people's technique of using a piece of flint and a piece of steel; an old file works very well. Hold one stone in your left hand (if you're right-handed), with your palm up, and place a ball of very fine tinder in that same hand: puffball spores, pulverized rotten wood, or pulverized birch fungus, for example. The inner bark of cedar will work, but it will need to be almost powdered. Strike the left-hand stone with another one in your right hand, letting the sparks drop onto the tinder until it starts to smolder. When it does, blow on it until you get a flame.

## The Wooden Fire Kit

Another device that a lot of Indians used was a wooden fire kit. It was shaped like a drill, which spun in a little hole on a piece of board. As the drill spun in the hole, it created friction, and the friction caused the wood to heat up. If the drill was spun fast enough and long enough, the heat would cause the powdered wood to start smoking, until finally a red spark would start to glow. There were several kinds of fire kits, but one common sort was used with a little bow that made the drill turn. This sort of fire kit has four parts. The first part is the drill itself, which is a stick about two feet long and about as thick as one's thumb. The second part is the hearth, which is a flat piece of wood placed on the ground, and which has a hole that the drill is fitted into. The third part is the bow, which has a string that wraps around the drill to make it spin. The fourth part is the socket, which is a little piece of wood, bone, or stone that holds the top of the drill steady.

If you want to make a fire kit, you need to look for the right kind of wood. Several different kinds of

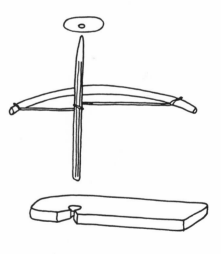

**4-1**
**wooden fire kit**

wood were used, but some are more useful than others. Sometimes the drill and the hearth were made out of the same kind of wood, but other Indians preferred to use a hard wood for the drill and a softer wood for the hearth. Quite often, the Indians used two good pieces of willow or poplar, which are fairly soft woods. Other good kinds of wood are pine or cedar. (There are several kinds of trees called "cedar"—eastern white cedar, eastern red cedar, western yellow cedar—they aren't really related to each other, but they all do well for making fire kits.) Other Indians of eastern North America used ash, oak, basswood, slippery elm, or sassafras wood.

The type of wood you use is important, but what is more important is that the wood must be dead and dry—very dry. Indians sometimes used rotten wood for the hearth, finding that this heated up more quickly than sound wood. They also often held the drill and the hearth over a flame before putting it away, finding that the charring made the drill work better the next time.

The drill is, as I said, about two feet long, and thick enough so that it won't bend as it spins. You could just make the drill out of a twig with the bark peeled off, but you can make a stronger drill if you split a log into quarters and then split out a piece of heartwood of the right thickness and whittle it to shape. In fact, it's better if the drill isn't rounded—give it flat sides, like the sides of a pencil. That way the bowstring will be able to grip the drill better without slipping.

The bottom end of the drill should be cut to a rounded shape, but leave it quite blunt. That's the part that will fit into the hearth, and you need it blunt so that it will rub a lot. The top end of the drill, however, should be cut to a fairly sharp point, because that's the part that fits into the socket, and you want that part to turn smoothly.

The hearth is a flat board about as long as the drill, two or three inches wide, and about half an inch or an inch thick. Like the drill, it should be split out of a log if possible, although it's true that a lot of hearths were made just by splitting a thick branch in half. Using a knife, drill a shallow hole very near the side of the hearth. Make the hole about a quarter of an inch deep, and about half an inch wide. This is the hole that the bottom of the drill is going to fit into. As you can see, the drill isn't going to go very far down into the hole. Then turn the hearth on its side and cut a big notch right into the side, so that the notch cuts right into the center of that shallow hole you had cut for the drill.

The socket, on top of the drill, can be any old shape, but it needs to fit comfortably under your left hand (if you're right-handed), and it needs to have a small hole underneath it to hold the sharp-pointed top of the drill. The socket can be made out of a piece of hard wood, perhaps a knot, but a piece of bone would be better. If you can find a smooth stone of the right shape, with a little hole on one side, you're in luck. I always keep my eyes open for pebbles that might have some future use as drill sockets.

The bow should be a bent piece of wood about two feet long, roughly the same length as the drill and the hearth. Some bows were made out of flexible wood, but a curved piece of a stiff dead branch is probably better. Cut a notch in a circle around each end of the bow, and fasten a cord to these ends. The cord needs to be strong, and a rawhide thong would be perfect. It should sag quite a bit, because it needs to wrapped around the drill.

Now that your fire kit is finished, you need some tinder to go with it. Once again the various trees called cedars are all useful; get some inner bark from one of these trees, preferably from a dead tree, and pull it to shreds or rub it between your hands until the fibers are well separated. You could also use the bark of white birch, either the outer bark, pulled into fine shreds, or the dark inner bark, used the same way. Pulverized rotten wood works well, and very dry grass or moss will work if you rub it enough to break it up somewhat (mouse nests and some bird nests are made of well-frayed grass). Some Indians pulverized various kinds of bracket fungi, which are hard growths that take the form of shelves or plates growing on the sides of trees; the kinds that grow on white birch were especially popular, and the wood where the birch fungus "roots" have penetrated also makes good tinder. Indians out west sometimes used the frayed bark of a kind of shrub which white people call big sagebrush. They also used the dried fibers of Indian hemp, which was also one of the main materials for making rope. A piece of cotton cloth that has been set on fire and stamped on (so that it is well blackened but not burned to ashes) makes good tinder material.

Put together some twigs for a fire, arranged in a teepee form, and have some tinder ready. Do this before you start trying to create a spark, because you'll be too busy afterward. Now put your fire kit together. Put the hearth on the ground, with the hole side to the right. Put a small piece of bark under the hole, to catch the spark. Put your left foot on the hearth to hold it down. Hold the drill in your left hand, and the bow in your right hand (if you're right-handed). Put the drill against the bowstring and twist it once around the string. The twist has to be the right way, so that the nearer half of the bowstring is higher than the other half, as you can see in the picture; if you put the twist in the wrong way, the string will rub against itself and eventually break. Put the bottom of the drill into the hole in the hearth. Then put the socket onto the top of the drill. You might also try putting a few grains of sand into the hole on the hearth, to increase the friction on the bottom of the drill.

Hold the bowstring with the tips of your fingers, so that the string grips the drill tightly. Start pushing the bow back and forth, so that the drill also turns back and forth. Keep the drill held down with your left hand, but use a moderate amount of pressure. If you don't press hard enough, you won't be able to create any heat, but if you press too hard, the drill won't turn properly. Keep sawing back and forth, keeping up a reasonable speed. If you go too fast, you're going to tire yourself out before you've created a spark, so don't overdo it. It takes a bit of practice to get the right motion, but if you've got it right, within a few minutes you'll see a thin gray wisp of smoke curling up from the wood powder on the piece of bark.

Don't stop yet, whatever you do. This first wisp of smoke isn't enough to start a fire, but if you keep going, the gray smoke will turn into a much thicker curl of black smoke, and this means that the center of the wood powder is actually starting to glow.

Now put down the bow and drill. Pick up the piece of bark with the burning powder and drop the powder into a wad of tinder. Blow gently on the tinder, so that the spark begins to glow more brightly. If you've got to that stage, it shouldn't be more than a few seconds before the tinder actually bursts into flames. As soon as that happens, put the tinder under the teepee of twigs in the fireplace and blow or fan the fire until it's going well.

One last word. Be careful with fire; it's far too easy to start a forest fire. Build a fire on bare rock or sand, not on vegetation. If you build a fire on grass or leaves, there's a chance that the flames could spread underground and flare up again much later. When you've finished with a fire, put it out properly, by dousing it with several potfuls of water. Pour on one pot, stir the coals up, and add the rest of the water. Once a campfire has been burning for an hour or so, it's amazing how much water it can absorb without going out, so don't underestimate how much water you'll need to extinguish it.

# 5

# SHELTER

There were many different kinds of dwellings built by the Indians. Some of them were meant for one family, and some of them were enormous, big enough for several families. Part of the difference had to do with the way people lived. Indians that were nomadic had to have small dwellings that could be easily put up and easily taken apart and carried, whereas Indians that stayed in one place all the time (or at least every winter) built larger houses.

Most Indian dwellings belong to one of three general types. The first type is the cone-shaped or dome-shaped dwelling, like the teepee of the Plains Indians. The second type was built in the form of a rectangle, with huge vertical posts that supported horizontal beams; these were the plank houses of the Northwest Coast Indians. Both of these types of houses were invented in Siberia by the ancestors of the Indians. Both might have a floor that was dug down to well below the surface of the ground, so that people could stay warmer—the birch-bark teepees of Canada often had a sunken floor, and even the floor of the Plains teepee was sometimes dug out. The third type of house was also rectangular and was probably invented in Mexico or South America.

Dwellings were built out of whatever materials were available: skin, bark, wood, stone, mud, grass, reeds—and the Eskimo igloo was built of snow. Some dwellings were just temporary shelters for an overnight camp, while others were built to last for centuries. Some were very simple in construction, others were very complicated.

## Simple Shelters

The simplest types of shelters are windbreaks and lean-tos. The Seri Indians, who lived on Siburon Island in the Gulf of California, didn't sleep under a roof of any sort, they just built semicircular windbreaks out of bundles of twigs. The climate was so warm, and there was so little rainfall, that they didn't really need anything else. The Paiute Indians of Nevada often lived in shelters that were no more complicated than those of the Seri. The Paiute dwelling was called a wickiup, and all it consisted of was three forked poles that were leaned together so that the forks interlocked, and then branches and bushes were piled against these three poles. Neither of these types of dwellings really provided much shelter, but it's worth remembering how to build such things, because in an emergency these shelters would be better than nothing. Even the Paiute wickiup would probably keep off a certain amount of rain, and both would protect you from hot sun or cold wind. If you've ever stood at a sheltered bus stop on a windy winter day, you may have noticed that keeping warm in the wintertime is often just a matter of staying out of the wind.

The Navaho Indians of the Southwest spent the winter in earth-covered dwellings called hogans, but in the summer they lived in much simpler structures, which were just lean-tos, built in any way that seemed convenient at the time. Lean-tos were built in many parts of North America, either for an overnight stay, or for an entire summer. Basically, a lean-to is a one-sided roof that touches the ground. There may be a short wall at each end of the lean-to, but there is nothing covering the front. Usually the campfire is built right in front of the lean-to, and the roof reflects the heat of the fire back onto the inhabitants of this dwelling, as well as providing protection against wind and rain. So it's a very simple design, but very practical. Designing a house in which one can have a fire burning merrily, without suffocating you with the smoke, isn't all that easy, but the lean-to is one solution to that problem. It's also a very easy thing to build, and you can take advantage of whatever sorts of materials you have in the immediate area.

One way to build a lean-to is to use a hatchet to cut down a small tree with a long straight trunk about four inches thick. You could use a dead tree for this, but if you do, place it between two logs on the ground and step on it to make sure it's still quite solid. Trim off the branches. Then look for two much larger trees, about ten feet apart and with branches coming off them about six feet above the ground. Place your log in the forks of these two trees, so that the log is now the main beam of your lean-to. You'll now need about twenty or thirty poles, each of them about ten feet long and about as thick as your arm. Lean these, all in same direction, with their tops against the main beam. For roofing material, find some dead birch trees or fallen logs and peel the bark off; bark from other kinds of dead trees will also do quite nicely. But be very careful if you're using birch bark: it catches fire very easily, so don't build a fire right in front of it. If you can't find bark, cover the poles with a thick layer of pine boughs or leafy branches, perhaps about three feet long. Add a few more poles on top of all this to keep everything in place, and there's your lean-to, ready to use.

If you like, you can give yourself a little more protection from the wind by using poles and boughs to cover the two ends of the lean-to. It's also a good idea to build the lean-to so that it faces east, since the wind is usually from the west (at least if you live east of the Rockies). If wind is really a problem, try to build the lean-to on the east side of a hill or on the east side of some large rocks or trees. But don't build the lean-to right under any trees, if you can help it; after a rain, those trees might keep dripping on you for ages.

This kind of shelter won't keep you bone-dry in a heavy storm, but it will keep off a light rain. What I often carry in the woods is a ten-by-twelve sheet of thick polyethylene. It's cheap, it's very lightweight, and it makes an absolutely waterproof roof for a lean-to. You have to be gentle with it, though, because the stumps that are left on the poles can easily puncture the plastic sheeting. When you put poles on top of the plastic to hold it down, don't just throw them on.

If you plan to spend the night in your lean-to, remember that a comfortable bed is very important. It's hard to enjoy the next day if you haven't slept properly. If you're far enough north to find balsam fir, use that for a bed; collect several armfuls of branches, none of them longer than three feet, and pile them up for a bed. Use one or two logs on the side of your bed to hold the branches in place if you like. If you can't find balsam fir, then cedar, pine, or spruce will work. Or use maple or oak branches, or whatever else is convenient. If you can find lots of tall grass or reeds or cattails nearby, then they will work very well also, although it might be best to spread them out to dry in the sun for a few days first. The Ojibwa Indians of the nineteenth century sometimes folded a large square of cotton in half and sewed up the sides to form a mattress, which they stuffed with dry grass or whatever was handy; perhaps they used some other material before cotton was available.

Put your sleeping bag on top of this bedding, roll up some of your clothes for a pillow (I sometimes bring an old pillowcase, and shove some clothes into this at night), and there you are, all ready for a good night's sleep.

## Northern Conical Lodges

In Ontario, Ojibwa and Eastern Cree hunters often made a winter hunting lodge entirely out of thirty or forty balsam or spruce trees about twenty feet long. They stripped off all the branches and then tied three or four of the trunks together near their tops and stood them up, spreading the bottoms out in a circle, then piled the other trunks around these to make a cone. Then they took the branches that they cut off and piled them up on the outside of the cone.

These branches were always placed with their cut ends upward, and the first row was around the lowest part of the lodge, the second row above that, and so on, so that the branches would shed rain or snow properly. This layer of branches was finally a foot or more thick, and it reached about two-thirds of the way up the lodge, but the top of the lodge was left uncovered so that smoke could escape. Inside the lodge, more branches were spread for sitting and sleeping on, and a cleared area was left in the center for a fire.

This was one of the simplest of conical lodges, but there were many other forms, with the Plains teepee as the finest example. Throughout Canada and the northern United States, conical lodges were built with all sorts of materials, including skin, bark, and even reed mats. The framework was pretty well the same for all sorts of conical lodges, usually beginning with either three or four poles as the foundation. Three poles give a more solid foundation than four poles (in the same way that a chair might rock, but a three-legged stool won't), but four has always been a sacred number to the Indians. In the Plains teepee and some other conical lodges, the three or four foundation poles were tied together, but in some other types of conical lodges the foundation was made by intertwining three or four tree trunks that had a natural fork at the top. Then more poles were laid in the crotches of the foundation poles. The covering was put on, and a few more poles were added to hold the covering in place. There might be anywhere between ten and forty poles in a lodge, and the poles could be anywhere between twelve and thirty feet long.

The conical lodge found over most of Canada was often covered with caribou hides, draped on in any way that would keep out the wind and rain, and then more poles were added to hold the hides in place. An equally common covering was birch bark, which was first cut into three-foot squares. Several squares were sewn together (sometimes with the inner bark of willow or basswood) to form a long strip, and a stick was sewn to each end of these strips to prevent

**5-1**
**northern spruce lodge**

the bark from splitting. A number of these strips were laid over the foundation, again in any manner that would keep out wind and rain, fastened with ropes, and then kept more securely in place by a few more poles. There was no real doorway to these simple conical lodges, but an opening was left in the bark covering; if the covering was made of hide, one flap could be raised to let people in or out.

A fire was built in the center of the lodge, and the smoke escaped through the hole at the top. To provide a little more protection from the rain, sometimes a rectangle of bark was attached to two long poles, and the rectangle could then be adjusted to cover or uncover the hole somewhat when necessary.

## Paiute Houses

Besides the primitive wickiups, the Paiutes also made bullet-shaped houses out of cattails or grass. To make a cattail house, you need about two dozen willow rods as the foundation. The poles should be about an inch thick and about twelve feet long. You'll also need many armloads of cattails, a few dozen more rods an inch thick but only about three feet long, and a few yards of rope, which might be just strips of sagebrush bark or thin willow twigs.

Draw a circle on the ground, about ten feet wide. Around the circle, dig a dozen holes a foot deep, and plant half of the long willow rods in those holes. Then tie a circle of three or four long rods around this framework, about three feet above the ground. Leave a gap between two of the vertical willows, for a doorway. Tie another circle of willow rods about two feet above the first circle, but go all the way around this time. Bring the vertical rods in toward the center a bit as you do this. Then bend the vertical rods even more toward the center as you tie on a third hoop. That's the foundation. To make the covering, lay three of the shorter rods on the ground, parallel to each other but about a foot apart, and spread an armload of cattails on them. Put more willow rods on top, placing them just above the first rods, and tie all the rods together in pairs; make sure the knots you tie enclose a few of the cattails. Lift

**5-2**
**Paiute cattail house** *(frame)*

this mat up and lay it against the side of the house, with the cattails vertical. Tie it in place. Make many more of these mats and tie them in place all around the house, and then tie another layer on above these, and then more layers, until the house is covered with these cattail mats. Later on, as the mats dry out, you'll need to add more layers, until the house is quite windproof and rainproof. The top, however, is left open as a smoke hole.

The grass-covered Paiute house is somewhat similar, but the foundation is made of a great many more willow poles planted in the circle. Several bands of willows are tied around these vertical poles, or interwoven with them. Then bundles of grass are fastened together by twining cords in and out among them, forming a "hula skirt." The "skirt" is lifted up and tied onto the foundation. And so the work continues, until the grass "skirts" completely enclose the sides of the house.

## The Navaho Hogan

The Navaho, who live in the southwestern United States, used to spend the winter in hogans, which were earth-covered versions of the cone-shaped type of dwelling. The foundation was made of five logs, usually of pinyon pine, with the bark peeled off. The logs were about eight or ten inches wide at the butts, and about ten or twelve feet long, although some hogans used for ceremonial purposes were made of logs twice this length. Three of the logs had a fork at the ends, and the other two were straight. The hogan always faced east, and so to place the three forked logs in the right position they were first laid out on the ground so that one pointed south, one west, and one north. They were then raised, planted firmly in the ground, and then leaned inward, so that their tops could be locked together at the forks. Usually three or four men raised these poles at the same time. Then the two straight logs were placed against the others, but these straight logs were kept almost parallel to each other. They were about two feet apart at the top, and about three feet apart at the bottom, facing east.

Now that the five foundation logs were in place, many more smaller logs and poles were placed all around the outside of the hogan, closing the gaps as much as possible.

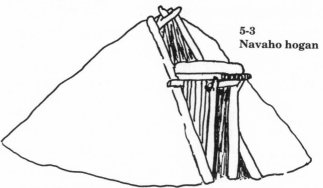

5-3
Navaho hogan

A doorway was built outward from the two long straight logs. This doorway began with two forked logs, about four feet long, planted in the ground just within the butts of the two straight logs, and a short log was laid between the forks. Another short log was laid across the two long straight logs, closer to the top of the hogan. Two long poles were laid between these two cross poles, and short sticks were then used to cover up the doorway roof. More sticks were planted in the ground to cover the sides of the doorway, and sometimes yucca twigs were used to tie these side sticks in place.

That completed the wooden framework of the hogan. A pit was dug about a foot deep inside the hogan to form a sunken floor. The pit wasn't dug all the way to the walls of the hogan; instead, a sort of bench was left all around, which was used as a storage platform.

The outside of the hogan was covered with cedar bark. The bark was covered all over with about six inches of earth, except for the very top, which was left as a smoke hole, and at that point the hogan was finished. Usually there were enough volunteer workers that a hogan could be started and finished in a single day.

The fire was built in the very center of the floor, as with other types of conical lodges. If the smoke got to be too much of a problem, people sometimes placed short logs horizontally to make a little four-sided chimney on top of the hogan.

## The Plains Teepee

The fanciest version of the conical lodge was the teepee of the Plains Indians, which was a portable dwelling made of buffalo hide (later canvas) stretched over a framework of poles. The whole affair could be taken apart and packed so that it could be carried by horses to another location.

Teepees were made with either three or four poles as the foundation. Roughly speaking, the Blackfoot, Crow, and other tribes of the far-western Plains used the four-pole foundation, while the Sioux and other tribes of the eastern Plains used the three-pole foundation. Teepee poles varied from 12' to 40' in length, but the average, at least in the nineteenth century, was around 20'. Smaller teepees needed fewer poles, sometimes as few as a dozen, while larger teepees would have thirty or more poles; the smallest teepees were used for hunting expeditions, while the largest teepees would be mainly for ceremonial occasions. Poles were valuable possessions, because long journeys were necessary to find the right kinds of trees.

Nineteenth-century teepees were larger than those of earlier times. Centuries ago, there really weren't many Indians living on the Plains, and they didn't have horses until after about 1650. Without horses for hunting and riding, it wasn't very easy to live on the Plains. And without horses to drag the travois (a sort of cart without wheels, made of two long poles that crossed over a horse's back), it was difficult to carry the heavy buffalo hide that was used for the teepee cover, let alone the poles that went with it. The early Indians used dogs to carry their small teepees, but even then it was necessary to divide a teepee cover into two parts, with one dog to carry each part.

Besides the poles, the various parts of a teepee include the covering, the door, the pins that fasten the covering together, and the pegs. The following

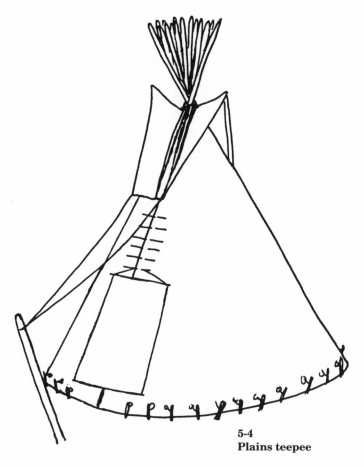

**5-4**
**Plains teepee**

describes the construction of a simple teepee with an 11' diameter, which is about as small as a teepee can get before you start to have real problems with smoke.

**Poles** You will need seventeen cedar, pine, or tamarack poles; cedar lasts longer, but pine is sometimes less tapered. (When pine was used, it was usually the species called lodgepole pine, *Pinus contorta*.) Tamarack is strong but heavy. The poles should be 14' long, 2–3" thick near the base, and 1–2" thick where they are tied together, 3' from the top end. Make sure they're well peeled, and that all knots are shaved down so that the poles have a perfectly smooth surface; a large drawknife is useful for this job. With a hatchet and a rasp, shape the bottoms of the poles so that they come almost to a point, for the last foot or so at the bottom. Tie all the poles together to make a rough teepee shape, and leave them outside for at least a few weeks, turning them occasionally. That will give them time to dry and harden, so that they won't sag when they're actually being used.

**Covering** The covering is made of cotton fabric; eight-ounce duck or medium-weight canvas is best. Lighter-weight material could be used, but it might not last as long. Nylon is of questionable value if you expect to build a fire in the teepee, since any spark will instantly create a hole. Whatever material you use, it should be light-colored, for the sake of a more cheerful appearance.

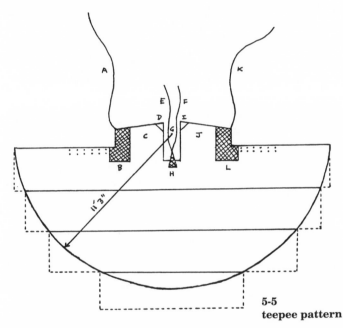

**5-5**
**teepee pattern**

If you use material that is a yard wide, you will need 72' (24 yards) of it for the cover. Cut it into one strip of 22', one strip of 21', one strip of 17' 8", and one strip of 11' 4". A certain amount of material will be lost when you make seams and hems.

The sewing can be done on a machine, or by hand. If you do it by hand, use a No. 6 or 7 needle, and the thread should be polyester, labeled "extra strong" or "for buttonholes or canvas."

Lay the material out in a back yard or on a large

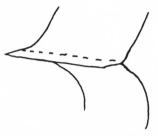

*a* sew edges together

*b* trim away edge
of one piece
of material

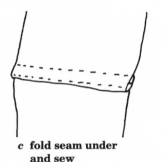

*c* fold seam under
and sew

**5-6**
**flat seam**

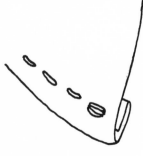

**5-7**
**hem with running stitch**

floor, cut the four strips to the right lengths, and line up the midpoints of the strips. Place two strips together so that the edges are facing in the same direction; use a few pins to help in lining things up. Put a running stitch along this edge, trim away the edge of the lower piece of material, fold the top piece under, and add a second row of stitching, creating a flat seam, as shown in figure 5-6. Make sure the outside of the seam points downward, like a roof shingle, so that the fabric will shed water.

To shape the bottom edge all around the teepee, get a piece of string slightly over 11′, and tie a piece of chalk to it. While someone holds the other end of the string a foot away from the long edge, at point G (in figure 5-5), run the chalk around the canvas to form the curve. Cut out the pattern.

Make hems all around the covering by folding the edges over twice and sewing them up with a running stitch (figure 5-7), back stitch, or (on a machine) straight stitch.

The smoke flaps should look somewhat like those in figure 5-5 (C and J), about 3′ long, and about 2′ wide near the center of the covering, with about a 1′ gap between them. To make these flaps, use material left over from cutting the main curve on the covering.

The holes for the pins that hold the front together go in pairs. Leave about 2″ between each hole and its partner, and there should be about 6″ from one pair to another. Cut a little ¼″ cross to make each hole, and use heavy waxed thread (such as No. 10 shoemaker's thread), sewn on with a buttonhole stitch (figure 5-8), to reinforce the edges of these holes. A buttonhole stitch is like an ordinary whip stitch (see chapter 6) except that just before each stitch is pulled tight, the needle is poked twice through the little "horseshoe" at the top. These holes start about 4′ from the outer curve, since the rest of the material is going to act as a doorway.

The smoke flaps need some triangular pockets sewn to them (D and I), to provide a seating for the two poles that will adjust the flaps.

Make the central tie flap (H-1′ × 6″), and the patches at B and L, from several pieces of scrap material sewn on top of each other, and run the stitching in a crisscross manner over these reinforcements, as shown in figure 5-5.

Sew a 6' cloth tape (E and F), bent in half, to the central tie flap.

Sew a 10' section of ¼" cotton cord (A and K) to the lower corner of each smoke flap; the best way to do this is to first make a hole, reinforced with buttonhole stitching, or to sew a small loop of cloth tape to the flaps.

**Door** Make a door by fastening a small rectangle of wool or cotton to two poles, or bend a stick into an oval and cut the material to the same shape. The door will be tied to one of the pins that holds the cover.

Soak the cover and the door in commercial waterproofing compound, enough to cover the 200 square feet of material. Any of the compounds you can find in a hardware store will do, although canvas doesn't last as long with mixtures that contain wax.

**Pins** The pins that close up the front of the covering are made of twigs—preferably dogwood, chokecherry, or ash—and are a little longer and thicker than an ordinary lead pencil. Leave several inches of bark on at the blunt end.

**Pegs** To hold the lower edge of the teepee in place, you'll need fifteen hardwood pegs about 1' long and about 1" thick. It's a good idea to leave the bark on, for a few inches at the top, so that the cord is less likely to slip.

**Erecting the Teepee** To erect the teepee, first lay the cover out flat with the inside surface facing up. Place two poles down the center of the cover, with their bottom tips just over the hem of the teepee. Place a third pole on top of these, pointing to the left. The crossing-point of the three poles should be right at the gap between the smoke flaps (figure 5-9). Tie the three together at that point, with the end of a 20' piece of ⅜" manila rope. The reasons for putting the poles on the cover first is to see exactly how far up the poles the knot should be. There were various ways of tying these three poles, but the Cheyenne method is shown in figure 5-10. Raise these three

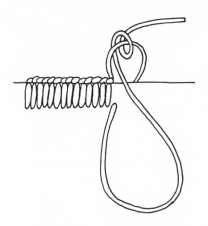

**5-8**
**buttonhole stitch**

poles and pull pole *b* toward you. It's very important that you pull this pole toward you, and not any other one. This way, they all lock together and support each other. If you move the poles apart the wrong way, one of them will end up sitting under both of the others, and they won't be supporting each other.

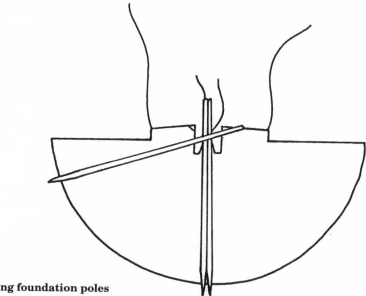

**5-9**
**aligning foundation poles**

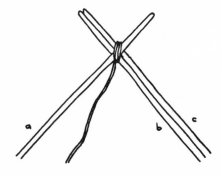

**5-10**
**tying foundation poles**
*(Cheyenne method)*

Make sure they face the right directions of the compass. As you can see in figure 5-11, one pole should be almost pointing east (though a little bit south), one should be almost southwest, and the third should be almost northwest. Move the poles out further, until they're nearly at the edge of an imaginary 11'-wide circle. The rest of the poles are placed in the crotch of the first three poles, in the order shown. First the space between the east and north poles is filled in, then the space between the east and south poles, then the space between the south and north poles.

Now take the end of your rope and walk clockwise four times around the poles, making sure that the rope is pulled up tight all around where they're touching at the top. Then wind the rope down the northern pole and fasten it with a half hitch. In really high winds, you might want to remove the

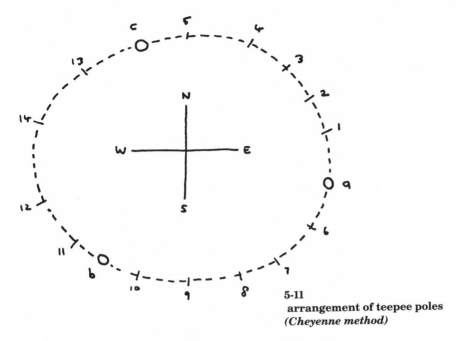

**5-11**
**arrangement of teepee poles**
*(Cheyenne method)*

rope from that northern pole and fasten it to a heavy
stake planted in the center of the teepee.

Now it's time to put the cover on. Put one of the
remaining poles on the teepee cover, again with the
bottom tip just over the hem of the teepee, and fasten
the center cords to that pole by cross-gartering
(figure 5-12); basically, you're spiraling the cords
around the pole, but one cord goes one way, the other
cord goes the other way. Tie them together at their
ends. Lift the pole and the cover onto the very back of
the teepee and wrap the cover around the poles.
Insert the pins to lace up the front. And now go inside
and move the poles out further so that they are
pressing against the canvas. Dig some small holes
for the poles to go into the ground.

Hammer the pegs into the ground, all around the
teepee. Get fifteen round pebbles about 1″ wide. Poke
each pebble into the canvas from the inside, then tie
a cord around the pebble from the other side and
then tie the cord to the peg (figure 5-13).

The last two poles are about 2′ shorter than the
rest. They are inserted into the pockets at the tops of
the smoke flaps. Rest the poles against the back of
the teepee, either crossing each other or with their

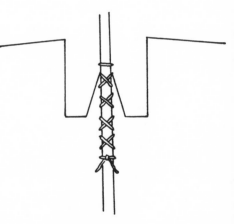

**5-12**
**fastening center
cords to pole**

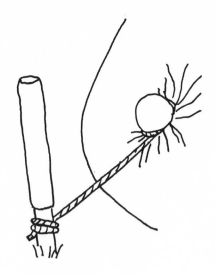

**5-13**
**attachment of peg**
**to teepee**

bottom ends touching. By moving these poles, you can modify the chimney effect of the top of the teepee, and in very wet weather you can move the poles around to the front so that the smoke hole is completely covered up. The long cords at the bottoms of the smoke flaps are attached to a small pole planted a few feet in front of the door, as you can see in figure 5-4.

Notice that the way the teepee cover was cut, the teepee ends up straighter on the west side (the back), and more slanted on the east side (the front). That way, the smoke can escape easily through the front poles, instead of having to go through the apex, where all the poles are tied together in a tight bundle. In addition, the slant makes the teepee better braced against the prevailing westerly wind.

Whenever you have a fire in the teepee, keep the door open, or leave a gap at the bottom of the cover, to allow air to flow in.

Most teepees were made more comfortable by providing them with an inner back wall, made of two blankets or pieces of cloth sewn together and fastened to the inside of the poles, and often the wall went all the way around the teepee. This inner wall served many purposes: it caught rainwater that dripped down the inside of the poles, it kept dew from falling on the people inside, it provided an air barrier for insulation, it protected people against drafts that blew under the cover, and by channeling those drafts it helped in pulling the smoke up to the top of the teepee.

If you're working with metric measurements, a similar teepee would have a 4m radius, with poles 5m long, and would be made of 28m of fabric, cut into four-meter-wide lengths: one of 8.2m, one of 7.9m, one of 6.9m and one of 5.0m. A radius of 4.1m should be drawn on the fabric. The other dimensions should be easy to convert (or estimate), remembering that an inch is 2.54cm, and a foot is .30m.

# 6

# CLOTHING

Indian clothing was generally cut very simply, even
though it might be highly decorated. Most Indians
dressed in clothing made from tanned hides. The
Eskimos and the Indians living just below the Arctic
Circle also used tanned hides, but their clothes were
cut into elaborate patterns, often involving many
pieces of hide, so that the clothes fitted the body very
neatly and provided comfort as well as great protection from the cold.

In the Southwest, clothing was woven from cotton
and (later) wool, on several kinds of looms. The
Indians of the Northwest Coast made capes, blankets, skirts, and a sort of dress-like man's garment
out of cedar bark, all woven on a primitive loom-like
device that was basically just three pieces of wood.
Many tribes of that area also made blankets from
mountain-goat wool, often adding dog hair, feathers,
fur, and other fibers. The Salish Indians, who also
lived on the Northwest Coast, had a loom that was a
little more elaborate.

Over a large part of North America, men wore a
long strip of buckskin, called a loincloth, between
their legs; it was about a foot wide and about five feet
long. The loincloth was held in place by a belt, and to
this belt were sometimes attached tube-shaped leggings that reached from the upper thighs to the
ankles. Buckskin shirts were used in Canada, but
were probably never worn in the United States

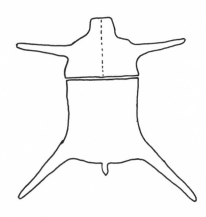

**6-1**
**hide cut for Plains poncho**

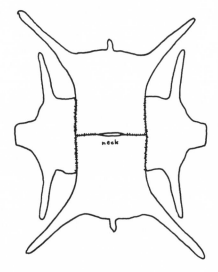

**6-2**
**poncho pattern**
**neck**

before white people arrived; instead, men usually wore a simple buckskin poncho in cold weather or on ceremonial occasions. Women wore long dresses made of two hides sewn together, or they wore wraparound skirts. They often wore knee-high leggings under the skirt or dress. Both men and women wore robes of fur or buckskin in cold weather.

The poncho that was used by men on the Plains was made from two entire hides of deer, antelope, or mountain sheep. Each hide was cut into two pieces, as shown in figure 6-1, and the pieces were rearranged as in figure 6-2, so that the two larger pieces became the front and back of the poncho, and the two smaller pieces covered the arms. The four pieces were sewn together, leaving a gap for the neck, but the sides were left unsewn.

Perhaps it was partly the influence of white men's clothing that led to the development of the true shirt among the Plains Indians in the nineteenth century, although Indian men further north had been wearing real shirts since long before that.

Some later shirts pretty well kept the original shape of the hide just as it came off the animal (as the poncho did), while other shirts modified the shape, so that the shirt ended up as more of a rectangle, like white men's clothing. And of course, the sides were then sewn up, and the underarms were sewn up to make real sleeves. That made a tighter-fitting garment, and often a slit was cut partway down the front of the shirt to make it easier to slip over the head.

The Plains woman's dress was also cut to avoid any waste of material. The dress was made of two entire elk hides, with the tails uppermost. The dress was sewn across the shoulders and at the sides, but the sewing didn't reach all the way to the underarms, so the garment was still somewhat open, like men's clothing. A belt was worn around the dress. Some people think that one or two centuries ago the women of the Plains only wore a hide wrapped around the waist, and that the full-length dress of two elk hides would have been rather a luxury in the days before guns and horses.

Usually the tail of the animal, along with a portion of the hind-leg area, was allowed to fall down to form a sort of yoke in front and back. The seam along the top then ran along this fold. There were modifications to this original form, so that the hide was sometimes cut in ways that didn't follow the original shape of the skin very closely.

Both men's shirts and women's dresses were often decorated with quills, beads, hair, shells, and other ornaments sewn onto them. The underarms, sides, and bottom edge were often cut into long fringes, or strips of fringe were sewn into the seams.

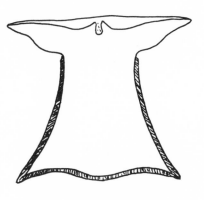

**6-3**
**Plains woman's dress**

The Pueblo Indians of Arizona and New Mexico (and later their neighbors, the Navaho) made their clothing from fibers woven on a loom. Because material woven on a loom has a rectangular shape, the clothing was also rather rectangular. Men wore a kilt, which was a rectangular piece of fabric wrapped around the body and held with a belt (also woven), and under that they wore a woven breechcloth. Sometimes they also wore woven shirts, which were somewhat like the Plains poncho; they weren't sewn at the sides or underarms, but there would be a few little strings on each side, which could be tied together to hold the garment onto the body.

The basic item of clothing for Pueblo women was very simple. It was a large rectangle of woven cotton or wool, about six feet wide and about four feet high, usually of dark material. It was wrapped around the body, under the left arm, and fastened over the right shoulder with a pin or with a couple of stitches. This dress was held in place by a woven belt.

Every tribe had its own way of making buckskin, but the process was usually somewhat as follows.

The hide was left to decompose slightly in water for two or three days, sometimes with wood ashes added to the water, until the hair began to loosen. A chisel-shaped bone tool with a sawtooth edge was used to scrape the flesh, fat, and membrane from the flesh side of the skin. A two-handed bone scraper, made from a sharpened rib or from a cut-away leg bone, was used to scrape off the hair. The black epidermis or grain, the outermost layer of skin, was also

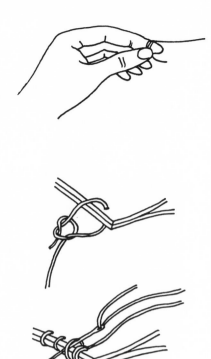

**6-4**
**starting sewing**

removed from this side; it is the removal of the grain that gives the suede-like appearance to buckskin.

The animal's brain was then mashed, mixed with a cup of water (or more), and simmered for a few minutes. The mixture was rubbed into the skin, especially on the grain side, and the skin was left for a day. Sometimes the hide would be repeatedly soaked in the brain mixture, wrung out, and soaked again. The brain mixture helped in softening the hide. In place of brain, other oily materials were occasionally used, such as liver or fat, and even ordinary cooking oil is sometimes used today. Sometimes the hide was thoroughly washed in clear water after the braining process, although other tribes omitted this step.

Then the hide was pulled and tugged and twisted for hours, perhaps by pressing it down over a sharp stake, until the material was as soft as velvet. The Ojibwa punched holes all around the hide, laced it to a rectangular framework, and rubbed the hide with a sort of spade-shaped stone tool.

When the hide had been well kneaded, it was sewn into a cone shape and suspended over a smoky fire for a few minutes or hours. The smoking ensured that the hide would stay soft even after it had been exposed to rain and sun.

Making buckskin is a backbreaking job, and if the hide has been left in water for several days it may have acquired quite an odor, so the process is not one that can be performed within city limits. Factory-tanned deer hide or moose hide is an excellent substitute for traditionally prepared hides, and ordinary suede from cowhide is suitable for many purposes.

The Indians used an awl to bore the holes for sewing leather. The awl was simply a pointed piece of bone; it might be made from the ulna, which is a thin bone in the front legs of large animals, or from any other small leg bone. The thread was inserted without a needle, although the Eskimos used small thin needles made out of bone. You'll find it much easier, however, to use a steel awl or needle than to use bone tools.

The thread was simply a strip of sinew, particularly deer sinew, taken from under the layer of fat along the backbone, or from the legs; it was dried, then pounded into individual strands. Sinew is very strong, and it is stiff enough that the tip can be easily inserted through a hole in the leather. For moccasins, however, some people preferred thread made from cedar bark, since it's less likely to fall apart in wet weather.

If you want to try sewing leather with an awl rather than a needle, you can use waxed dental floss as a substitute for sinew. The texture and stiffness are very similar. Other kinds of waxed thread can also be used with an awl. Making moccasins with just an awl and waxed thread isn't much harder than with a needle.

But if you'd rather use a needle and thread, one of the best kinds of thread is 68 percent polyester and 32 percent cotton. The label on the spool will say "extra strong." This kind of thread is often called button thread. Nylon thread tends to twist badly, and linen thread might not be strong enough.

I should mention some of the general rules of sewing. When you thread your needle, have about six inches sticking out past the eye of the needle, so that the thread won't keep falling out. Pull the other end of the thread off the spool until you've got about two feet unrolled, and then cut it; that'll give you enough to work with, but not so much that it'll keep getting tangled up in what you're doing. Keep a thimble on your middle finger so that you can push the needle without injuring yourself.

When you're making your first stitch in a piece of work, run the needle and thread through the same hole three or four times; you can improve on this technique if you run the needle under each of these three or four stitches just before you pull it tight, as shown in the bottom picture in figure 6-4. This is the one of the best ways of starting a line of stitching, since it involves no knots; thread or string tends to break at a knot, since the fibers are cutting across each other.

But it's also possible to begin a line of stitching by

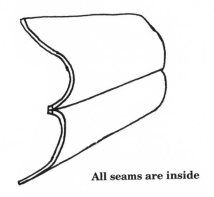

**All seams are inside**

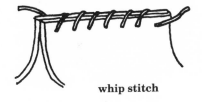

**whip stitch**

**running stitch**

6-5
**sewing buckskin**

**selvage strip added**

**cut into main material**

**6-6**
**sewing fringe at a seam**

one of two other methods, which are quite effective for cotton fabric, especially where the sewing is not going to be pulled too much—at a hem, for example. These other methods make the thread less conspicuous.

One way, shown at the top of figure 6-4, is to wrap the thread two or three times around your finger, and then to brush your thumb forward over the thread, so that it all balls up at your fingertips. Hold the main part of the thread and then pull on that ball you've created. It forms itself into a tight irregular lump. When you start sewing, that lump will prevent the start of the thread from coming out of the fabric.

Another way of starting a thread is shown in the middle picture. Run the thread almost all the way through the first hole, then tie an overhand knot in the end. Slip the needle through the knot, and pull the thread tight.

To *finish* a row of stitching, use the same technique that I first mentioned for starting a row: run the needle through the same hole three or four times, catching the previous stitch each time.

The two stitches that were most often used for sewing were the running stitch and the whip stitch. (These both have several other names in English.) Most sewing was done with the edges of both pieces of material facing the same way, and the material was reversed when the item of clothing was being worn, so that the stitches were invisible. The whip stitch is much stronger than the running stitch, and I highly recommend that you use it for most sewing. The only slight disadvantage is that the stitches are a little more visible than with the running stitch. With moccasins, one way of avoiding this problem is to insert piping, a narrow strip of leather, between the two pieces of material; the thread then goes through three layers instead of two.

# 7

# MOCCASINS

On their feet, men and women generally wore some kind of shoes, which we now refer to by the same native word that many Indians used: moccasins. There were a great many kinds of moccasins, but many of them resembled the two types we are going to look at: the side-seam moccasin and the puckered moccasin. Moccasins were usually made of deer hide, but several other kinds of animal skins were used at times.

To make moccasins, you'll need about three square feet of leather. If you buy half a hide you'll have enough for several pairs of moccasins, and you'll be able to be a little more choosy about what sections to use. Unless you're using suede or Indian-tanned hide, the leather will have two different sides. The smooth, outer side is what we call the grain side, and the rough side is what we call the flesh side. The difference is important when we come to putting together the various bits of the moccasins.

The needles should be glover's needles, which are three-sided, although you could use an awl and waxed thread if you prefer. You'll need some pieces of paper for making patterns; paper grocery bags are good for this. Other items you'll need are a thimble to protect your fingers, a large pair of scissors, a ruler, a measuring tape (a piece of string will do nearly as well), and a ballpoint pen or (preferably) a fine-tipped felt pen.

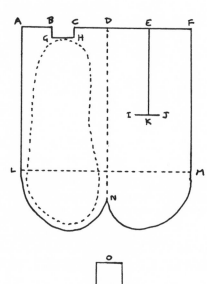

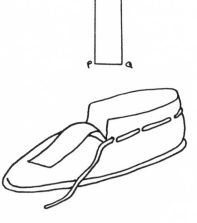

**7-1**
side-seam moccasin

Indian moccasins were always sewn inside out, and then turned "outside out" when the sewing was finished. That way all the seams ended up on the inside of the moccasin. The kind of moccasins you see in a modern shoe store aren't like that; they're generally made with an exposed seam running around the toes. If you want to make the puckered type of moccasins, and all you have is ordinary cowhide or suede, you'll have to ignore all the instructions about sewing moccasins inside out; sew them outside out, with all the seams exposed (and don't use any piping).

Never use anything but a whip stitch when sewing moccasins, because it's much stronger than a running stitch.

Make moccasins so that they fit fairly tightly, because the leather will stretch as you wear it. If you're using heavy leather, add about 1/4″ to the length and width of the pattern to allow for the thicker seams.

See the previous chapter for notes on sewing techniques.

## Side-Seam Moccasins

The easiest kind of moccasin to make, and one of the most comfortable, is one that isn't seen very often nowadays, although it was made by Indians in many areas. This type of moccasin was made from basically one piece of hide, with the main seam running all around the outside edge of the foot. Side-seam moccasins were made with definite rights and lefts, unlike some other kinds. For side-seam moccasins, you can use any kind of leather, as long as it is fairly soft, and thin suede works very well.

On the paper, trace the outline of your foot. Then wrap a measuring tape or a piece of string around the widest part of your foot, just behind your toes. That length should be transferred to the paper to give you the line LM in figure 7-1. Then draw around your foot outline, so that you add 3/4″ at the heel (BG and CH) and 1/2″ extra at the toes; that's for a full-size adult foot, but don't add so much if your foot is smaller.

In the heel section, BG is 3/4″, and GH is 1 1/2″.

The slit EK should be half the length of DN. Make the slit IJ about 2″ wide. The tongue is a rectangle the same length as EK and the same width as IJ.

Cut out the pattern. Fold it in half along the line DN and trim the edges to make both halves identical. Use a pen to trace the pattern onto the flesh side of a piece of leather. Try to have the center line, DN, going from the left side of the hide to the right (or vice versa), not from the front legs of the hide to the back legs. If you don't have a whole hide to work with, it might not be easy to figure out which way the hide originally went. If so, don't worry about it.

Flip the pattern over and put it on another piece of leather to make the second moccasin.

Cut out the all the pieces of leather. Put one of the main pieces on the ground, with the grain side facing up. Fold one side over and sew the whole thing up from N to A (not A to N, because you might need to make adjustments), using a whip stitch. If you're using deer hide or moose hide, keep the stitches about 1/8″ apart. If you're using cowhide, you might have to keep the stitches 1/4″ apart. Sew up the heel end by joining AB to CD, and sew up what is now a horizontal slit at GH. When you've finished, turn the moccasin inside out—or perhaps "outside out" is a more accurate way to say it.

Put the tongue on top of the moccasin, with the grain side down. Point O of the tongue should be touching E, P should be touching I, and Q should be touching J. Lift up the edge IJ slightly, lift the edge PQ the same way, press them together, and sew them together with a whip stitch.

If you want to add tie strings, get a round piece of fairly strong scrap leather about five or six inches wide and cut it into a spiral. If you're using cowhide or moose hide, make the strings 1/2″ wide. If you're using deer hide, make them a little wider for strength, perhaps 3/8″. Pull the material tight to straighten it out. Punch the holes for the tie strings in the positions you can see in figure 7-1. You can start the holes with a steel awl, but you'll need something thicker to finish them: perhaps a large

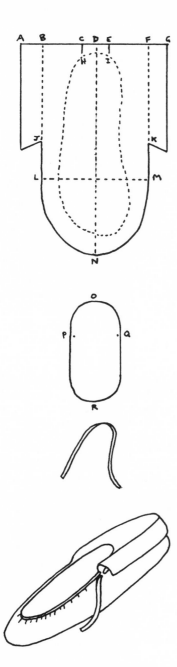

nail or a Phillips screwdriver (the kind with a cross-shaped tip). The original bone awl would be just about perfect for this job. You could always cut horizontal slits if you prefer, and with thick leather you might have to do that, but slits on thinner hide might tear eventually.

## Puckered Moccasins

Another type of moccasin has a seam that runs all around the top of the foot. This second type has a bottom piece, which is basically the sole, and an upper piece, the vamp. The sole is folded up toward the top of the foot, and around the toes it has to be puckered—gathered together—so that it can be sewn onto the vamp. With this type of moccasin there is no difference between the moccasin for the right foot and the one for the left foot.

For puckered moccasins, you have to use deer hide or moose hide, because you need a material that will pucker easily. The hide doesn't have to be Indian-tanned (smoke-tanned), because commercially tanned moose hide and deer hide are just as soft. But cowhide and horse hide are too stiff, no matter how thin the material may be (unless, as I said, you keep all the seams on the outside), and pigskin is too weak. You can buy deer hide and moose hide in most large stores that sell leather. The commercially tanned hides will cost you about twice as much as cowhide; the Indian-tanned hides might cost you a great deal more, at least if you buy them from a store.

Trace the outline of your foot onto a piece of paper, as shown in figure 7-2. Don't follow the outside of your toes precisely, because this outline will be used for both your feet. Then draw lines BJ and FK; they should be about half as long as the center line DN, and an inch away from sides of your foot, but they must be the same distance from the center line. As with the side-seam moccasin, you should add 3/4" to the back, and HI should be twice as long as CH. The front end, however, should be long enough so that when you turn it back it will reach the base of your big toenail. The flaps on the sides, extending from A to B, and from F to G, should be an inch wide.

**7-2**
**puckered moccasin**

The vamp, the oval part that goes on top of the moccasin, is about half as long as your foot. The two points P and Q are about two-thirds of the distance from O to R.

The width of the vamp is a bit tricky. It's based on the measurement you got from the widest part of your foot. That measurement must be equal to LM added to PQ. So if, for example, the distance around the widest part of your foot is 10″, and if LM is 6″, then PQ must be 4″. The vamp is straight along the sides, and rounded at both ends.

Cut out these patterns for the sole and vamp. Fold the paper along the center line DN and make sure both halves are exactly the same. When the patterns are properly trimmed, trace them onto a piece of leather, and cut them out. Use exactly the same patterns to cut out the leather for your other foot.

Another piece you're going to need is piping, which is a thin strip of leather, 1/4″ wide, which will go right into the seam when you sew the vamp to the sole. Its purpose is to prevent the stitches from showing when you turn the moccasin right-side out. Take a circle of leather about four or five inches wide and cut it into a spiral. When you've finished cutting it, pull it tight to straighten it out. For each moccasin, you'll need a strip that is the same length as the distance around the vamp from P to R to Q.

Now you're going to sew the vamp to the sole. But the outer edge of the vamp, the curve from P to R to A, is much shorter than the curve on the sole from J to N to K. You know that you'll have to pucker up that curve, but how can you do it so that you end up with it looking neat and even?

Here's one way of doing it. You can use a pen to place dots on both pieces of leather, to show where the needle should go through. The number of dots in the vamp must be exactly the same as the number of dots in the sole. The only difference is that the dots in the vamp are going to be closer together than the dots in the sole.

So begin by using your pen to make three dots on the flesh side of the vamp, at P, R, and Q. Make a dot between P and R. Make a dot between R and Q. Make dots between each one of *these* dots. And then make dots between each one of *those* dots. Keep going in that way, so that the dots are always the same distance apart. When you've made enough dots that they are now only about an 1/8″ apart, you can stop.

Remember: the number of dots on the sole has to be the same as the number of dots on the vamp. So count the number of dots in the vamp. Then mark a dot on the grain side of the sole, right at the front, at point N. Put another dot at point J, and a third at K. Then start making more dots between each of these points, but keep track of how many dots you're making. Stop when you've made the same number of dots as you had in the vamp.

Put the sole on the ground, grain side up (i.e., with the pen marks showing). Put the vamp on top of the sole, flesh side up (and so again with the pen marks showing), with R, the tip of the vamp, on top of N, the tip of the sole. Find the midpoint on that strip of piping, and place it, grain side up, under the vamp, sandwiched between R and N.

Now you're ready to start sewing. We start by tacking the vamp to the sole, so that we can see where we're going. Take a few inches of thread and sew it through N and R. Make sure that the piping gets caught between the vamp and the sole. Go through two or three times and cut the thread. Fasten P to J in the same way, and then Q to K.

Now for the puckering. Put about two feet of thread on your needle and shove the needle through the vamp, the piping, and the sole, close to N. Use those pen marks to see where your needle should go. Keep sewing (with a whip stitch) along that edge until you get to J (or K), and then do the same along the other side. You may need to use your fingers to encourage the sole to pucker up as you sew: squeeze the sole into little pleats, so that the holes on the bottom stay in line with the holes in the vamp. When you've gone all around the front of the moccasin, run the thread through the last hole several times to keep it from unraveling.

Sew up the heel end of the moccasin by joining AC to EG. Turn the moccasin right side out. Turn up the heel flap and sew it in place. By the way, when you're doing an area like that, don't just make one hole, running your needle all the way into the moccasin, and then make another hole from the inside, to bring the needle out again; that way, it's hard to see what you're doing. Instead, pinch the leather and shove the needle through two holes at once.

If you don't want to be bothered with sewing up heel flaps, you can just cut them off, as we did with the side-seam moccasins.

And now you're all done, except that again you may want to punch holes around the ankles so that you can insert a tie string.

## Quills and Beading

The Plains Indians used to decorate their moccasins (and other clothing) with porcupine quills. The quills were dyed and flattened, and the ends were tucked under and sewed down with sinew. The quills were sewn side by side in this manner to form a pattern over the top and sides of the moccasins. But for the last century or two, the Plains Indians also got European beads from traders. The beads were sewn onto the moccasins with either of two types of stitch: the lazy stitch and the overlay stitch.

The lazy stitch was the most commonly used type of stitch, and it was done by putting about six to ten beads onto a thread and sewing them all onto the moccasin with one big stitch. Then a tiny sideways stitch was made, and another six to ten beads was sewn down next to the first bunch, and so on.

The overlay stitch was a bit harder to do. Several beads were strung onto a thread, and both ends of the thread were knotted so the beads didn't fall off. The threaded beads were placed on the moccasin, and another thread was used to sew the first thread in place, but these stitches went between each bead, or at least every two or three beads, so that they were held in place more firmly than with the lazy stitch.

The lazy stitch was faster, but the overlay stitch was better when there were a lot of curves in the pattern. It's usually easy to see the difference between moccasins decorated with the lazy stitch

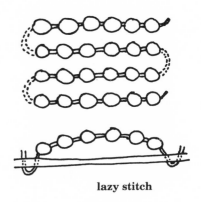

**lazy stitch**

**overlag stitch**

7-3
**beading**

and moccasins decorated with the overlay stitch, because with the lazy stitch, the big loops in the stitching make the beading look as if it's carved into ridges, like a plowed field.

Different tribes had different types of patterns in their beadwork. Sioux moccasins tended to have a lot of background, usually rather light colored, and the designs tended to be rather spindly and spread out. The Crow Indians' moccasins were quite different: the Crow liked to use large triangles and diamonds, and sometimes the background was made of red velvet instead of with beads. The third common style was that of the Blackfoot Indians, who tended to make patterns of diamonds, triangles, squares, and diagonal bars, but what was unique about these patterns was that they were actually made up of tiny parallel squares. The Eastern Woodland Indians preferred fairly realistic patterns of flowers and leaves.

# 8

# WEAVING

It is hard to say exactly which Indian tribes practiced weaving, because it all depends on how you define the word. Some looms were hardly more than a piece of wood or string from which to hang the fibers that were woven. Also, weaving was not used only for clothes: the same sorts of techniques were used for weaving baskets and mats and other things. But in this chapter we shall be looking at the weaving of clothing. There were basically two groups of Indians that regularly made woven clothing, and those were the people of Washington state and British Columbia, and the people of Arizona and New Mexico. Often it was blankets that were woven, but these blankets were mainly regarded as clothing, not something to put on a bed.

We shall be looking at three types of looms, the Salish loom, the Pueblo tubular loom, and the Pueblo blanket loom. Each one is more complicated than the last. I suggest that you start by building a Salish loom. If you can do some nice work on that, go on and build yourself the next type of loom. If that doesn't seem too complicated for you, you might want to go on to the Pueblo blanket loom.

## The Salish Loom

In British Columbia and Washington, the Salish Indians wove beautiful blankets out of a variety of materials, but they mostly used the wool of mountain

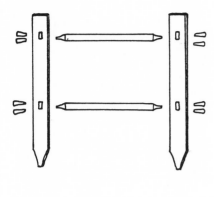

**8-1
Salish loom**

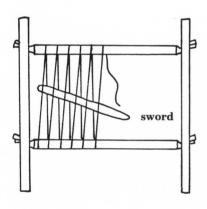

sword

goats. Sometimes they shot the goats for meat and then used the wool for weaving. The female goats left a lot of wool in the beds where the young goats were born, up in the hills, and this wool was collected in the late spring. And when the goats shed their winter coats they left tufts of wool on all the bushes.

Often the entire blanket was made of mountain-goat wool. For other blankets, the wefts (horizontal strands) were made of mountain-goat wool, but the warps (vertical strands) were made of the twisted inner bark of red cedar, or of nettle fiber or Indian hemp. Sometimes the mountain-goat wool was mixed with other materials: dog hair, the fluff from milkweed pods, the similar fluff from fireweed seed-pods or from cattails, or even feathers, strips of bird skin, or fur. The Salish Indians have been making their own types of blankets again in the last few years, but now they generally use ordinary sheep's wool.

To build a Salish loom, you will need two boards about an inch thick, about four inches wide, and about three feet long, although the actual size doesn't matter very much. You will also need two round poles about an inch or two in thickness and about four to six feet long. Cut the ends of the poles almost to a point, but leave them nearly half an inch thick at the ends. The two boards need to have a couple of rectangular holes cut all the way through them, and for this you will need a drill or a chisel; cut the holes a little bit over half an inch wide, and about an inch long. Figure 8-1 shows what the pieces should look like. The loom was originally stuck in the ground, and that is why the boards are shown pointed at the bottom, but if you intend to use it inside you might want to just cut the boards straight at the bottom.

Besides the two boards and the two poles, you will also need about eight small wedges to hold the whole thing together. The wedges should be cone-shaped, but square-ended ones will work fairly well.

To beat the thread into place, you'll need a sword, a flat stick about two feet long and one or two inches wide.

Set up the loom by standing up the two boards and putting the two poles between them. Jam the wedges into the holes to keep everything steady. Tie the loose end of a ball of wool yarn to the bottom pole and wind the yarn around and around both poles in a sort of spiral, but keep the turns of the yarn close enough that they are touching, not loose as the picture shows (which is just to indicate how the spiral looks). When the two poles are completely covered with wool, tie the end down in the same way it was tied at the beginning.

Now it's time to start the actual weaving. With the Salish loom, the first row of weaving is always at the top of the loom, and the work continues downward, whereas in most other kinds of loom weaving, the weaving goes from bottom to top. There are two general kinds of stitches used with Salish weaving: twilling and twining (figure 8-2). Twilling involves passing the weft thread under two warps, then over two warps, then under two warps, and so on. When you reach the end of the row, keep going in the opposite direction, but everything is shifted over by one stitch, so that the under-two stitches aren't exactly under the ones in the previous row.

There's an easy way to keep the very beginning of your weft thread from sticking out. Lay the thread in among the warp threads, a few inches from the edge, and then weave it toward the edge before you turn back and start weaving the first row. The very last row of weaving is finished in a similar way: just poke the thread in between the last row and the second-to-last row for a couple of stitches.

Twining (figure 8-2) is different from twilling in several ways. The very first weft thread is bent in half, so that both halves are woven into the warps. When either half starts to run out, we just lay another thread parallel to it. Most importantly, the two weft threads are twisted every time we go from one warp thread to another—they keep crossing each other's tracks. And thirdly, we usually don't skip over two warp threads the way we do with twilling.

Always work with a piece of thread about as long

twilling

twining

8-2
Salish weaving

as your arm. That's long enough to keep you going for a while, but not so long that it'll keep getting in the way. When you run out of thread, start another piece near the first one, but overlapping the first thread for an inch or two. If you keep all your stitches well packed together, it'll be impossible for anyone to see where one thread ends and another begins.

It is always important to keep the sides of your work even. The stitches should be packed together well from bottom to top, of course, but make sure that you aren't pulling the sides toward each other. If you start doing that, you'll end up with the middle of your blanket narrower than the ends. You've got to keep the blanket the same width at all times, and the only way to do this is to be gentle with those weft threads, especially when you reach the end of a row and are reversing the weft thread to start another row: don't pull the thread.

When you've woven the weft yarn back and forth enough to cover all the area between the two poles, it's time to pull out the wedges and turn the two poles, so that your woven material goes over the top pole and down the back side of the loom, leaving you with more unfilled warps. Jam the wedges back into place to keep everything steady, and continue with the weaving until only about three inches of the warp is left uncovered with weft thread.

When you've finished all the weaving, you'll have produced a sort of flattened tube of wool. Now take a pair of scissors and cut through those warp threads that you left unwoven. The whole piece of weaving will fall off the loom. Tie those loose threads together in pairs, so that your work won't unravel, and there you have your first piece of Salish weaving.

As you may have guessed by now, it's possible to do all sorts of interesting things in making patterns. In the first place, the stitches can be varied tremendously. If you're using twilled weaving, the under-two stitches have to shift over with each row, so that the weaving has a slanted look to it. In fact, twilled weaving is sometimes called diagonal weaving, but that's bit confusing because there's also a technique in weaving baskets where the threads actually run diagonally, so we'd do best to keep to the name twilling. But the point I was trying to get to is that the apparent slant that is caused by shifting the stitches over can be reversed every few rows, so that all sorts of zigzags and diamond shapes can be created just by changing the stitching.

The other way to create patterns in your weaving is by using thread of different colors. Some kinds of Salish blankets were mostly white, with just a few thin colored stripes along the edges, but others were quite colorful. The patterns were made up of stripes, zigzags, squares, rectangles, triangles, and diamonds. Draw your pattern on a piece of paper, using colored pencils or felt pens, and follow this pattern as you weave. Each time you need a new color, just cut off the previous thread and weave the end back under the previous row, and then begin with your new color. One thing you have to watch out for, however, is that the patterns mustn't continue vertically for too long, because a vertical line means a slit in the material. You're changing from one color to another, and there's nothing joining them together. It's all right to do that for a few rows, but it shouldn't go on too long. The trick the Salish weavers used was to break up those vertical lines one way or another. For example, instead of weaving a vertical stripe, they would weave a vertical row of small squares, with the squares separated by a row or two of the background color.

The Salish loom is a pretty primitive device, and it's rather a slow job to weave on it. But don't despise it. For creating elaborate patterns, the Salish loom is perhaps better than any other type of loom, simply because the work is done one stitch at a time.

## The Pueblo Tubular Loom

The Pueblo Indians of the Southwest, and the Navaho, used what is sometimes called the "true loom." It is called that because it was made in such a way that the Indian worker ("he" or "she"—both men and women were weavers in the Southwest) could do a whole row of weaving in one motion, whereas with the Salish loom, every stitch had to be done individually. The Pueblo Indians also used a different material: cotton. After the Spanish introduced sheep to the area, however, they also made clothing from wool.

Two or three different kinds of looms were made, from narrow ones for making belts, to larger ones that are nowadays called blanket looms, which were used for clothing.

A common Pueblo loom was the tubular loom shown in figure 8-3. The four big pieces of wood around the outside can be made of two-by-fours nailed or screwed together, but for the side pieces the Indians actually used forked posts stuck in the ground, and the top and bottom pieces would be heavy poles tied to the forked posts. If they were working inside a house, they might not use side posts at all, but instead they would simply hang the loom from one of the log beams that ran along the ceiling. Most of us don't have log beams across our ceilings these days, so two-by-fours will have to do. This kind of loom was mainly used for narrow pieces of weaving, so the form should only be about two feet wide at most, although it can be five feet high.

Before work begins on the loom itself, the top and bottom loom poles are tied to two temporary side poles (figure 8-4), so that the warp can be strung on. Tie the warp to the bottom pole and then bring it up to the top pole and down again, and so on, around and around the two poles in a great spiral. Keep each length of warp thread just touching the previous one.

Now the top loom pole is held up by a cord that is fastened to the top of the frame, looped around, and finally brought down to the side of the frame and tied. The purpose of this cord is to hold up the top pole, of course, but it's also to keep tension in the weaving. The warp threads have to be kept tight, and as the weaver fills up the loom, the threads pull everything a bit tighter, and so the top cord will then have to be loosened.

The bottom pole is loosely attached to the bottom of the frame by two loops of cord.

Untie the two temporary side poles and put them aside.

Two thin sticks, a and b, are pushed through the

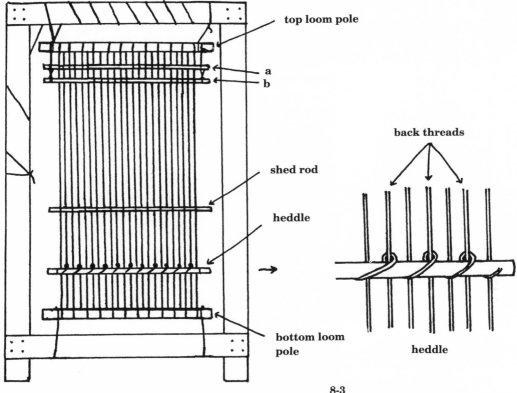

top loom pole

a
b

back threads

shed rod

heddle

bottom loom
pole

heddle

8-3
Pueblo tubular loom

top of the warp to keep the threads from wandering around all over the place. They are tied to the top pole by two loops of cord that are twisted slightly, as shown in figure 8.3.

Now comes the big difference between the Pueblo loom and the Salish loom. The Pueblo loom has two very important little sticks that speed up the weaving process enormously. There are several names for them in English, but often the bottom one is called a heddle, and the top one is called a shed rod. These two rods are used to pull forward a number of warp threads all at one time, so that the ball of weft thread can be passed behind them, and a whole row of weaving can be done in one movement. When the shed rod is pulled, all the front threads are pulled forward. When the heddle is pulled, all the back threads are pulled forward.

The shed rod is placed between the front and back

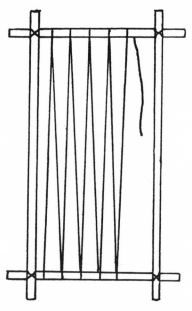

**8-4**
temporary frame for Pueblo tubular loom

warp threads, as you can see in figure 8-3. But the heddle stays in front of all the warp threads; it is attached to the back warp threads by winding a string all along it.

Another big difference between this loom and the Salish loom is that the weaving was always done from bottom to top, not from top to bottom. The first length of wool was passed between the two rows of warp threads, and then the heddle was pulled forward so that the wool could be brought back in the opposite direction, going *under* the same threads that it had gone *over* in the first row.

The sword was used to beat each weft row into place, and to hold the two rows of warp apart when inserting the weft thread.

When the weaver had woven enough rows to completely fill the front of the loom, the big cord at the top of the frame was loosened, and all the weaving was pulled down and around the bottom pole, so that the weaver had a whole new area to work on. When this area was nearly filled, the last few inches of warp were cut all the way across, and the weaving came off the loom. The result was a very long but rather narrow piece of weaving, perfect for a belt—which is a typical product of these looms. Peruvian Indians used these looms for blankets, though: they made several of these narrow strips and then sewed them all together.

## The Pueblo Blanket Loom

Now we come to a rather more complicated type of loom, a big loom that was used for weaving blankets by about half a dozen different tribes in the American Southwest. Like the tubular loom, the blanket loom was also used with a temporary frame to string the warp threads into place, but the process was a bit more complicated. Let's go over the stages in more detail.

The first step is to make a rectangular frame of four heavy poles. You might want two poles about six feet long, and two side poles about five feet long. Place them on the ground and tie the corners together tightly to make the temporary weaving frame (figure 8-5).

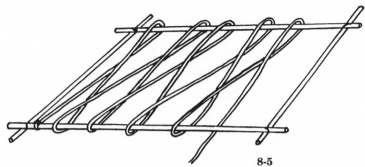

8-5
temporary weaving frame for Pueblo blanket loom

Now we need to make the loom itself (figure 8-6). You'll need a frame of some sort, either two-by-fours nailed together, or two forked posts planted in the ground, with two posts tied between them to form a rectangle. You'll also need three smaller poles to hold the weaving: in figure 8-6 these are called the top loom pole and the bottom loom pole, and a third (which I call the adjustment pole) is needed above those, to hold the long spiral of rope that can be loosened or tightened to give the right tension in your weaving. Then you'll need two even thinner rods for the heddle and the shed rod. Besides all that, you'll need some rope to hang the weaving onto the frame, and strong cord for the sides of the blanket.

Start the weaving process by putting the warp thread onto the temporary weaving frame. We start the same way we started with the other two types of loom, by tying the warp at the bottom left corner. But now there's a big difference. We don't just loop the thread around and around the top and bottom poles (or near and far poles, since it's still all on the ground). Instead, we wind it back and forth in the form of a series of figure eights, as shown in figure 8-5.

Now take about fifteen feet of strong cord, fold it in half, and run both halves along the outside of the top pole, twisting it once (or two or three times, if the cord is thinner than the wool of the warp) between each loop of the warp, as shown in figure 8-7. This cord is called the top selvage cord.

Do the same at the bottom, twisting a selvage cord between all the warp threads on the outside of the bottom pole of the temporary weaving frame.

The third step involves one of the actual loom poles—one of the poles that are going to hold your work when the actual weaving begins. Fasten it to the top selvage cord with a spiral of cord (figure 8-8). Do exactly the same at the bottom, with the bottom selvage cord.

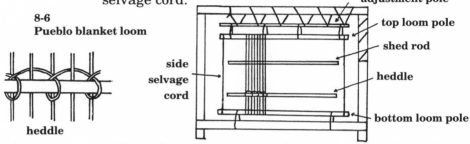

**8-6**
**Pueblo blanket loom**

heddle

adjustment pole

top loom pole

shed rod

side
selvage
cord

heddle

bottom loom pole

Now that these two poles are attached to the selvage cords and the warp, you can dismantle the temporary weaving frame: untie it at the corners and slip it all out from the warp threads and put it aside.

You're now ready to put the warp and its two poles onto the frame of the loom. All you need is one last pole, the one called an adjustment pole in figure 8-6. Fasten it to the top loom pole with about half a dozen separate loops of cord. The adjustment pole is fastened to the very top of the weaving frame with a long zigzag of cord, the tension cord, identical to the tension cord that is used with the Pueblo tubular loom.

Fasten the bottom loom pole to the bottom of the weaving frame with a few more loops.

All that's left is to slide the shed rod into place near the top of the loom, and fasten the heddle onto the warp near the bottom of the loom. The reason I say "near the top" and "near the bottom" is that those warp threads cross halfway down, since we fastened them on in a bunch of figure-eight loops; the warp threads that are in front at the bottom aren't the same as the threads that are in front at the top.

The Pueblo weaver also fastened a cord to each side of the loom, next to the two sides of the warp. These cords are called side selvage cords. In fact, sometimes there were two or three cords touching each other on both sides of the warp. When you start weaving, just run the ball of wool in and out, around these cords, before starting back in the opposite direction. The cords are to strengthen the sides of the blanket.

Weaving on the blanket loom is almost identical to weaving on the Pueblo tubular loom. Again you pull the heddle toward you, pass a ball of wool between the two rows of warp until the ball comes out at the other end, turn it around, pull the shed rod toward you, and pass the ball of wool back the other way.

One big difference is that once you reach the top of the loom, you don't pull the warps down and start over again. There's only one side with this sort of loom. But the nice thing about this loom is that you can do much bigger pieces of work: a whole blanket, all in one piece.

Because you can't go all the way around the warps in tube fashion, you find yourself running into a little problem. When you get close to the top of the loom, you'll find that there just isn't room to finish the job. The heddle gets in the way, the shed rod gets in the way, and the warp and weft threads are all too close to each other. There are two solutions to this problem, and the Indians used either method. One solution is to take out the heddle and the shed rod and just weave the weft thread in and out of the warp, one stitch at a time, almost like sewing. That way you'll be able to get pretty close to the top of the loom, before you have to untie everything from the loom.

The other solution is to stop weaving when you get halfway up the loom. Then turn your loom upside down and again weave from the bottom to halfway up the loom. That way you'll end up with the very middle of the blanket left unstitched, and again you'll have to pull out the heddle and the shed rod and put those last few rows in by hand.

When you're working on your blanket, remember

**8-7**
**top selvage cord**

**8-8**
**fastening loom pole to selvage cord**

the rules: keep everything even, and keep your sides straight so that you don't end up creating an hourglass-shaped blanket. Use your sword to knock all the threads into the right position.

You might want to avoid patterns with your first blanket, or keep the pattern fairly simple, but later on you can try something fancier. To change colors partway along a row, just don't let the ball of wool go all the way; pull it out from the warp threads and put another ball of wool in its place. Another trick is to have more than one heddle. Each heddle is fastened to a different bunch of warp threads. But leave all that until you've had a bit of practice making plainer blankets.

## Spinning

One day you might want to try spinning your own wool or cotton, if you can get raw material. Try to start with wool, since it's much easier to spin than cotton.

Wool was cleaned and straightened out somewhat, and twisted on one's thigh to form a very loose sort of thread that modern weavers refer to as roving. The length of roving was then spun on a spindle. The spindle was a rod about two or three feet long, usually pointed at the top, with a whorl (disk) of wood or stone or other material jammed onto it about a third of the way down. The Indian method of spinning involved two stages (after the roving had been spun). To begin with, the loosely twisted roving was tied to the spindle just above the whorl, and the lower end of the spindle (below the whorl) was rolled down the top of the worker's thigh so that about three feet of roving was coiled up on the rod. The second step was to hold the spindle still, and to pull those three feet of thread off the rod (leaving the very beginning of it still tied to the rod, of course), but pulling it in such a way that the thread is pulled parallel to the rod. It is this second, pulling process that actually puts the twist in the thread, strangely enough. Try it and see.

And that's really all there was to the spinning process. After the thread had been pulled off the rod, it was coiled up again above the whorl, and another three feet of thread was started.

The Southwestern Indians liked to keep their yarn quite thick, and the yarn spun for a blanket would be about a quarter of an inch in diameter. However, the first time the yarn was spun, it would probably be rather lumpy and irregular, so after a few feet had been rolled onto the spindle and then stripped off again, the spinner would jam the spindle under his foot and go over the thread, pulling out the thicker portions and letting the spiral run up them to even out the whole length of thread.

After the entire length of thread had been spun, it might still be too loose by Indian standards (Indian thread was generally spun more tightly than modern wool thread, especially if it was being used for the warp), so the entire ball might be spun all over again, as much as four or five times.

Long before the Indians of the Southwest had wool, they used native cotton. It was grown in the fields, along with other kinds of crops. When each cotton plant ripened, it produced a big wad of fluff which we now call a boll. The bolls were collected, but they were full of seeds, which had to be picked out by hand, one at a time. However, one trick of getting rid of the seeds was to put the bolls between two blankets and then beat the blankets with a stick, so that the seeds fell out and left the clean cotton fluff behind. When the cotton was free from seeds, it was pulled roughly into long strands. Sometimes a small wooden comb, with only two or three teeth, was used. The fibers were brushed with the hands into a long roving, and the roving was then spun into thread with a spindle.

## Dyeing

To dye wool or cotton, there are usually two things needed: a dyestuff, which is some sort of plant or mineral material to provide the color, and another material that we call a mordant, which makes sure the color won't wash out later, or get bleached out by the sun. A few kinds of dyestuffs don't need mordants. No one is really sure about all the different kinds of dyes that the Indians used, or how they used them. But in any case, dyeing is a matter of experimentation, and the Indians were always trying new methods. You can dye the raw wool or cotton before you spin it, but you can also use dyes for coloring fabrics after they've been taken off the loom. It's generally easier to dye wool than cotton.

What you might find really useful is two very large enamel pots, and a big wooden spoon.

For mordants, the Indians often used human urine, or they used a naturally occurring form of alum called alunogen, a mineral that is sometimes found in the Southwest. Another important mordant was the tannin that occurs in the bark of many kinds of trees, and so if these barks were also used to color the wool or cotton, nothing else would be needed to fix the color. Iron and copper were also used in early times, both as mordants and as coloring substances; the iron would come from certain kinds of black mud, or from a crumbly red or yellow stone called ochre, which is just iron oxide. The copper would have been far more rare, but Indians in some areas found veins of pure copper, or they used copper sulphate. Iron tends to darken colors. The Navaho also burned the green needles of juniper for a mordant; the ashes from plant material are a natural source of alum.

Nowadays there are several modern chemicals that are used as mordants, especially alum (available in most grocery stores and drugstores), although chrome (but stay away from it—it's quite poisonous), tin, and copper sulphate are also used. Cream of tartar (also available in most grocery stores) is often used with these mordants.

Chop or crush the dyestuff as much as you can, and use *lots* of it, because natural dyes are less powerful than synthetic ones. Add just enough water to cover the material and let it sit overnight.

Here's how to add the mordant to one pound of wool. Before you use the mordant, the wool has to soak in water for about an hour, because wool absorbs water very slowly. Then dissolve half a cup of alum and two tablespoons of cream of tartar in about two cups of boiling water, and pour this mixture into four gallons of cold water. If your tap water is hard (contains lime), add about a cup of vinegar to soften it. Add the wet wool and bring it all slowly to a boil, then let it simmer for about an hour, and then let the wool cool in the water, or lift it out with the wooden spoon and let it cool.

While the wool is cooling, strain your dyestuff. Tie up the solid matter in a cloth and put it back into the water in which it sat overnight, and then add enough water to make four gallons. Bring it to a boil and let it simmer for an hour. Add the wet wool and let it simmer for another hour, and then take it out and let it drain.

In olden times, the Salish Indians used the shells of hazel nuts for a brown color, the bark of alder for red, a plant called wolf lichen (*Evernis vulpina*) for yellow, and fern roots for black. They also got black from the inner bark of hemlock or birch, boiled with iron-containing mud or (later) in an iron pot.

The Navaho had many natural dyes for wool; most of the plants they used are only found in the Southwest, however. They got a yellow dye from several sources: the flowers of a type of rabbit brush (*Bigelovia graveolens*), the leaves and twigs of shad scale (*Atriplex canescens*), the flowers and twigs of chamiso (*Chrysothamnus latisquamus*), the twigs and blossoms of another type of rabbit bush (*Chrysothamnus bigelovii*), the flowers and leaves of owl's foot (*Helenium hoopesii*) or owl's claw (*Hymenoxys metcalfei*), the roots of canaigre (*Rumex hymenosepalus*), or the entire plant of bitter ball (*Tagetes micrantha*). They made a reddish-brown dye by mixing the inner bark of a type of alder (*Alnus incana*) and the inner bark of mountain mahogany (*Cerocarpus parvifolius*). Another brown came from the leaves, hulls, and whole nuts of the black walnut tree (*Juglans nigra*). The bark and berries of a type of juniper (*Juniperus monosperma*) supplied a green dye. Orange came from the leaves, stems, and flowers of Navaho tea (*Thelesperma subnudum*). The fruit of a type of prickly pear, *Opuntia polyacantha*, supplied a beautiful pink dye, but it is said to be not very long-lasting. Purple came from the roots of wild cherry (*Prunus cerasus*). Red came from the roots of wild plum (*Prunus americana*), or from the leaves, twigs, and berries of sumach (*Rhus trilobata*). Black came from a combination of three things: the leaves and twigs of another type of sumach (*Rhus aromatica*), yellow ochre (the soft iron ore mentioned earlier), and the gum of pinyon pine (*Pinus edulis.*)

A great many more plants will supply dyes. The hulls (the rubbery outer layer covering the nut itself) of walnuts, butternuts, pecans, and hickories will give a good brown dye without a mordant, and the shells or whole nuts are also worth trying. The inner bark of white birch, hemlock, alder, and balsam fir (and probably many other trees) gives orange or brownish shades without a mordant. Most green plant material will give a green dye, but might need a mordant. Lots of berries give red or blue dyes, but again might need a mordant.

# 9

# MAKING ROPE

**S**tring and rope were used for making almost everything, and the Indians had all sorts of fibrous materials that were suitable, but there were only two general ways of converting those fibers into a finished piece of cord. Most string was made by *twisting* strands of fiber together, like the ordinary cotton string we use today. At other times, string was made by *braiding*: the sort of technique we use to put pigtails in somebody's hair. Other kinds of material, however, were neither twisted nor braided, and were just used as single strands.

## Materials

One useful rope plant that grows mainly in the southwestern United States is yucca, also called Spanish bayonet, mescal, or century plant. Some Indians boiled the leaves with a handful of wood ashes to soften them and separate the fibers. Other Indians chewed the leaves and spat out the juice. The fibers might be further separated by gently banging the leaves with a rock.

Another southern plant that provides long fibers is agave, also known as maguey. But be careful. Agave will cause a serious burning sensation in the mouth, so don't chew the leaves, just boil them to separate the fibers.

Further north, basswood and willow both have inner bark that provides good thread for fiber. The best time to gather the bark is in the spring, when it separates easily from the outer bark and the wood. Soak the inner bark in water for several days, or boil it for an hour or two, again adding wood ashes if you have any, until the fibers separate. And the Indians knew that a thin willow shoot can be used as a sort of "rope" just by itself, with no further treatment.

The Ojibwa (Chippewa) of Minnesota and Wisconsin used the stem fibers of false nettle (*Boehmeria cylindrica*). The plants were gathered in the autumn and hung up to dry. When they were to be used, they were soaked for a few days, then beaten with sticks until the fibers began to separate.

In the west, the inner bark of western red cedar and various kinds of maple were used for rope and string. The Indians of the Canadian west coast used the entire bark of bitter cherry, cut from the tree in a spiral around the trunk. The inner bark of silverberry and the entire bark of big sagebrush (*Artemisia tridentata*) were used in the northwestern United States and in British Columbia. In the east, the inner bark of eastern white cedar, mulberry, leatherwood, and slippery elm were used.

In most of what is now the United States, a smaller plant that was often used for string was Indian hemp (*Apocynum cannabinum*). The plants were collected in the autumn, after the frost had killed them. The leaves were pulled off, and the stalks were gently crushed and split. The outer skin and the inner pith were both pulled off and discarded, leaving the long thin fibers. Dogbane and milkweed, both related to Indian hemp, were used the same way. Don't chew the fibers of Indian hemp or dogbane, since they're both somewhat poisonous when raw; raw milkweed isn't especially good for you, either.

The strongest string was made of sinew, and so this is the material that was most often used for bowstrings. Sinew is just another name for the tendons, the white threads inside the muscles (the meat) of an animal. There are some fairly long tendons in the legs of large animals, but the longest ones are buried under the fat that runs along the backbone.

# Twisting

Take about a dozen strands of any sort of fiber. Unraveled wool or string will do. Keep some more fibers nearby, because you'll need them later. Lay that first bunch of fibers together side by side. Fold the bundle of threads in half to form two bundles. Hold your left hand palm upward (if you're right-handed) and pinch the folded part of the bundles between your finger and thumb. With your right hand, twist about two inches of the closest bundle of threads clockwise as tightly as you can get it, and then hold that twisted part down with your middle finger—it's a little bit like trying to play a guitar. Then twist the other bundle of threads the same way and hold that down with your ring finger.

Now that you've got both bundles tightly twisted clockwise, you need to twist those two bundles together around each other. So carefully push the two twisted bundles next to each other and pinch them together at the lowest part of the twist. Let go of the top of the bundles, the part held with the thumb and index finger of your left hand. The two bundles now spring together with a counter-clockwise motion. If you've done all that properly, you've now got two or three inches of good string, tightly bound together and not likely to unravel.

How does that work? Because you've got two forces operating against each other. The individual threads are twisted together clockwise, but the two bundles have sprung together counterclockwise. The two forces fight against each other and so everything remains locked together.

Poke those first two inches of finished string up between your left forefinger and thumb, pinch it tightly, and repeat the process. Always keep the twisting tight; that's the secret of success. If the two bundles start getting a bit sloppy, pull them away from each other to make the spiral run further up the string.

Eventually you'll start running out of fiber. As soon as one bundle starts looking a bit skimpy, lay some more fibers in place and keep going. When your

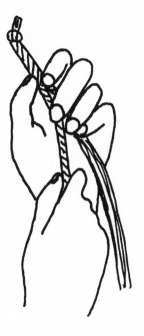

**9-1**
**twisting**

**9-2
braiding**

string is long enough, tie a knot in the end to keep the ends from fraying.

## Braiding

Braiding does not produce as strong a rope as twisting, and it is a slower process, but it is a good technique for materials that are slippery or otherwise difficult to work with, such as horse or buffalo hair. Rawhide was also often braided, especially for making snares for big game. Most braiding was done with three strands of material. To braid rawhide, for example, take three long rawhide thongs, tie them together in a knot, and fasten the knot down somewhere, perhaps by driving a nail through a board. Lay the three strands out side by side.

Place the left-most strand to the right of the center strand. Place the right-most strand to the left of what is now the center strand. Place the left-most strand to the right of what is now the center strand.

And so on. It's all a process of continually bringing the outside strands in toward the middle. Try it for a while, and you'll see what I mean.

## Using Sinew

If you know a hunter or a butcher, see if he will help you pick out the tendons from a carcass before it is cut up. When you get the tendons, lay them out to dry, and then pound them gently with a smooth rock until they separate into fibers. Split the fibers apart with your fingernails, until you've got them divided into fairly fine thread. Don't wet the sinew at this point, because you shouldn't soak out the natural glue, which you'll need when making the string.

Sinew strands were sometimes twisted, by the usual technique, but for small jobs the strands were used with no treatment other than being held in the mouth for a few seconds to soften them.

## Using Rawhide

A second animal material was rawhide. Thongs were made by cutting a circular piece of wet rawhide into a spiral. Rawhide was treated to all three methods: sometimes the individual thongs were used just as they were (but first wetted slightly, to soften them); at other times two thongs were twisted together; and at other times (particularly when making snares for big game) the thongs were braided.

## Using Tree Roots

Spruce root is one of the easiest kinds of rope to procure. Any kind of spruce will do: white, black, Engelmann, Sitka. If you don't have any spruce in your neighborhood, look for jack pine, or lodgepole pine, or western red cedar, or tamarack. If you're short of all of these needle-bearing trees in your area, willow roots will do quite nicely. (There are three sources of rope on a willow: the inner bark, the roots, and the entire shoots). Poke around in the ground beneath the tree, and you'll find plenty of roots; they run along just under the surface. Look for roots about as thick as a pencil, but thicker or thinner ones may be just as useful. When you've found the root, cut it off close to the tree, and then just lift it out of the ground. Get a good armful, because there will be a certain amount of waste. Don't just take them from one tree; take a few from each tree, wherever the picking seems good. That way you'll find the roots more quickly, and you won't be doing any harm to the trees.

Starting at the thick end, peel the bark off the roots. You may need to soak or boil them first, or you could just scorch them over a fire. The bark comes off fairly easily, but you could end up with a sore thumbnail afterward, so you might want to use a small knife for the peeling.

When you've got all the bark off, split the roots in half, again starting at the thick end. You may find that sometimes the split goes off to one side before you reach the end of the root. To prevent this from happening, when the split starts to wander to one side, bend the piece of root on the *other* side downward a bit more sharply. That will pull the split back to where it's supposed to be. Let the roots soak for several hours before you use them. Hot water will speed up the soaking period.

Tree roots were mainly used for sewing up objects

made of birch bark. When the roots dry, they are very hard and stiff, so they are ideal for sewing bark, but that kind of stiffness would be unsuitable in rope for other purposes.

When you're threading the root through the holes in a piece of bark, make sure that the shiny, smoother side of the root is on the outside. That's the part of the root that was closest to the bark. By keeping the shiny side outward, the root will bend more easily, it will be less likely to fray, and it will also look nicer.

# 10

# BASKETS AND POTTERY

**B**askets and pots were important to the Indians; they used these things to collect, carry, and store food, and sometimes even to cook food. Baskets were made out of a great variety of materials: the inner bark of willow, maple, "cedar" (all sorts), or juniper; the entire bark of sagebrush; the peeled (and usually split) shoots of willow, hazel, western red cedar, sumach, cottonwood, mulberry, blueberry, or acacia; the split stems of reed, rush, or cane; the split leaves of cattail, yucca, or agave; corn husks; and the split roots of spruce, western red cedar, pine, sedge, or rush—just to name the most popular materials. Later on, white settlers in the eastern United States taught the Indians how to make baskets out of splints: long thin strips of ash, oak, or hickory wood.

Hard materials such as twigs made fairly stiff baskets. Softer materials such as inner bark or cattails made more flexible baskets. Sometimes these softer baskets were really more like bags than baskets, and in fact the inner bark of the trees I mentioned above was soft enough that it was also used for making rope, mats, and clothing.

There were many materials, and an even greater variety of basket designs. But the above list may give you some idea of where to start looking for materials if you want to make your own baskets. Or you might

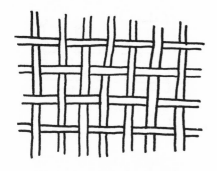

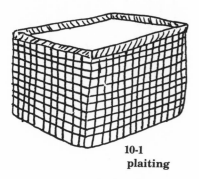

**10-1**
**plaiting**

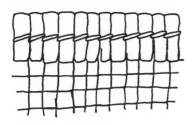

**10-2**
**rim for soft plaited material**

**10-3**
**rim for plaiting or twining**

want to start with commercial reed, cane, and splints from a crafts store.

The materials were usually collected, prepared (peeled, debarked, split, or whatever) and allowed to dry, and then moistened slightly when it was time to make the basket. The reason for letting the material dry first, after collecting it, is that if it were used fresh, it would shrink too much later, and the basket would fall apart.

When the material was about to be used in making a basket, it was only soaked long enough to make it flexible, but not so long that it would absorb a lot of water—and then shrink later, when the basket was finished.

There were three ways of making baskets: plaiting, twining, and coiling. Some of these methods have already been discussed in chapter 8. Plaiting is the easiest technique to learn and is generally the quickest way of making a basket.

## Plaiting

Plaiting (figure 10-1) is basically an over-and-under process, although there are many variations of this. You could, for example, skip over a couple of stitches every time, to create an over-two-under-two kind of weave (called twilling) instead of the usual over-one-under-one. The strands that run straight up the basket are called spokes, and the strands that run from side to side are called weavers.

Plaited baskets often had square bottoms. A number of strands of material (usually inner bark or split twigs) were woven together until a wide enough bottom was created, and the strands were then bent straight up to begin the sides of the basket.

One of the peculiarities of plaiting is that you always have to have an odd number of spokes. If you don't, the weavers will just keep going under the same spokes every time around. There are two ways to solve the problem: either skip over one of the spokes when necessary, or insert another spoke into the basket.

When you've reached the top row of weavers, you'll

need some way of finishing the rim. For a soft material such as cedar bark, the top ends of the spokes are bent straight down into the inside of the basket, fastened with a string or strip of bark twined around under the last weaver, as shown in figure 10-2. For stiffer materials such as willow twigs, bend the tops of the spokes sideward and hook them under each other (figure 10-3), or poke them down into the weavers (figure 10-4), or bind a split willow rod all around the rim (figure 10-5).

Many kinds of plant material were used for plaiting, but split willow twigs, split cane, split yucca leaves, and the inner bark of cedar were all very popular, in the various areas where they were found.

## Twining

Twining is somewhat like plaiting, except that the weavers are a pair of strands, not a single strand, and the pair of strands is given a half twist every time it goes around a spoke.

Unlike plaited baskets, twined baskets usually had round bottoms, with the spokes coming from the center in a star pattern. There are many ways to start a twined basket, but a common method is shown in figure 10-6. Four spokes are laid together to form a cross, and the first weaver is bent in half and twined all around them. The twining continues around the spokes several more times, forming a spiral. When the first weaver runs out, another weaver is laid next to the end of the first one, and you keep going. (You only fold the first weaver in half, not the rest of them.)

Eventually the stitches start to become too wide, and so you must add more spokes. Just poke one into each of the four corners. Continue your twining until you again need to add more spokes. Gradually draw the sides of your basket upward, so that you are forming a bowl shape. Three ways of finishing the rim are shown in figures 10-5 to 10-7.

Many kinds of plant material were used for twining, but the split roots of spruce and pine were used quite often, while other tribes used the twigs

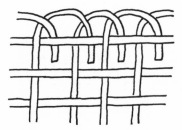

**10-4**
**rim for plaiting or twining**

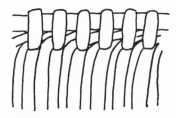

**10-5**
**rim for plaiting or twining**

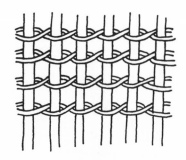

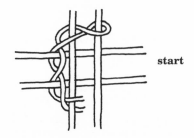

start

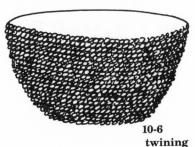

**10-6**
**twining**

from various trees and shrubs, such as willow, cottonwood, or hazel. Often the spokes were made of stiffer material than the weavers, and so unsplit peeled twigs might be used for the spokes, while split twigs were used for the weavers. Flexible baskets and bags were made from such materials as corn husks, cattail leaves, or sagebrush bark, for the spokes, perhaps with Indian-hemp string (see chapter 9) for the weavers.

## Coiling

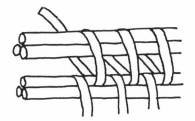

Coiling (figure 10-7) is quite unlike plaiting or twining: a foundation, consisting of one or more rods (often three), or of a bundle of fine material, is built up in a great spiral, and some sort of thread is used to sew the spiral together. An awl is used to help in inserting the thread. The thread has to be quite flexible, and so it is usually made of a finer material. One way of starting the basket is shown in figure 10-3: the thread is wrapped several times around the very beginning of the foundation material, the foundation is bent into a spiral, and the thread is wrapped around it. Unless the foundation consists of a single rod, the basket might be made with some variation on the basic stitch: the thread might pass over only two of the three rods, for example, or the thread might pass through part of the bundle instead of going around it.

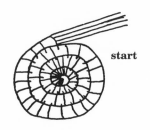

start

Coiled baskets don't really need any special technique on the rim, but often the rim was bound with a spiral stitch.

In British Columbia, coiled baskets were made with the finely split roots of western red cedar for both the foundation and the thread, although juniper and cedar roots were sometimes used. The Hopi used grass stems or shredded yucca leaves to make a rather thick foundation, and split yucca leaves were used for the thread. But in most of the southwestern United States, the foundation was made of three peeled rods of willow, or sometimes of cottonwood or squawberry (*Rhus trilobata*); thread was usually made by splitting willow twigs into three parts, using the teeth and both hands.

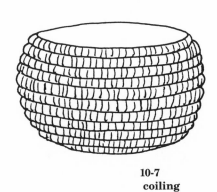

**10-7**
**coiling**

# Birch-Bark Containers

The Indians of eastern Canada made a great many things out of birch bark, and by that I mean the bark of the white birch, sometimes called canoe birch, a tree with pure white bark. The Indians traveled in birch-bark canoes, they often slept in birch-bark lodges—which were made in several different shapes—they lit fires with pieces of birch bark, and they kept all sorts of things in birch-bark containers.

Before you start peeling bark off a tree, though, make sure you have permission. If you peel the bark from all the way around a tree, the tree is going to die. If there are many white birches in your area, the loss of one won't be too bad, although it would be best if the tree could be cut down and the wood put to some use before it rotted.

Or find a dead birch and peel off the bark. When a birch tree dies, the bark lasts a lot longer than the wood. The wood turns black and rots away, and the hollow sleeve of bark is left behind. But if you can find a birch that has not been dead for too long, you may find that the bark is still quite usable.

The bark peels more easily in the late spring. In the middle of winter, it won't peel at all, unless you pour hot water over it. (Sometimes the Indians did peel the bark at this time, because they believed that winter bark was stronger.) Make a vertical slit in the trunk for as long as you like, and then ease the bark away from the wood. You might want to use a short pole shaped to a chisel edge, as the Indians did, in order to separate the bark from the wood. You should use the bark as soon as possible, while it's still flexible, and keep it out of the sun so that it doesn't dry before you've finished making something with it. If you don't have time to use it right away, it can be stored, but keep it flat, and weigh the corners down with heavy objects so that it doesn't curl up. Stored bark will dry out, but if you soak it for a while it will become flexible. Holding bark in front of a fire also makes it flexible, but be very careful: birch bark burns so rapidly that it's almost explosive. It's wonderful for making fires—but sometimes you don't *want* to start a fire.

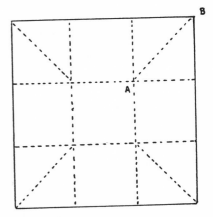

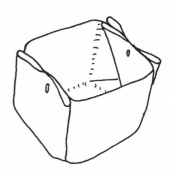

**10-8**
**simple birch-bark container**

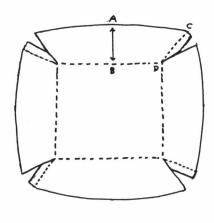

**10-9**
**birch-bark dish**

Birch bark is used inside out: the brown inner side becomes the outside of the container, and the white outer side becomes the inside of the container. Peel off a layer or two from the white side, though, to get rid of loose stuff.

Birch bark is fairly tough material, tough enough for making canoes that could hold a dozen or more passengers, but when it dries out it has a terrible habit of splitting along its grain. So whenever it is being bent into shape, it must be handled carefully, and it must not be allowed to dry out while it is being cut and sewn. When the container (or canoe) is finished, the bark can then dry to a wood-like hardness with no danger. The result, in fact, is a product with a remarkable combination of strength and lightness.

A simple birch-bark container is shown in figure 10-8. Make sure your bark is quite flexible, either because it's fresh or because you've given it a good soaking. This container can be made in a matter of minutes, and yet because it is made of a single folded sheet of bark, it is watertight, and in fact it was placed under maple trees to collect sap.

Mark the square of bark as shown in the top picture; fold line AB up toward yourself, and do the same at the other three corners. Don't crease the folds too much, or the bark will split.

Bend the folds together on two sides, so that you end up with a cube shape, and use an awl to poke a few holes so that you can put in one or two stitches of split spruce root.

The northeastern Indians made an attractive dish-like container, used for all sorts of things. Find a piece of bark that you can cut in the pattern shown in figure 10-9. You'll also need a thin willow branch, about four times as long as the container, to use as a rim, and a few feet of split spruce root for sewing. The dotted lines in the drawing don't represent lines that need to be folded or cut; they're just there to help you see how to draw the design. The line AB is the same length as the line CD, and for that reason the outside curve isn't exactly a circle, but a sort of rounded square. After drawing all the outside curves of the pattern, draw the notches at the corners. Notice that a little tab is left in each of these corners, so that you have something extra for sewing the seams. Cut the pattern out, and sew up the corners with spruce root, making sure that all your materials are well soaked.

Peel the bark off the willow shoot and split it in half, saving the best half for the rim of your container. Dump this willow into the water, along with the roots.

Let the willow soak for a few hours, and then wrap it around the top of the container for a minute, to see how long the piece of willow should be. Cut it so that it's about two or three inches longer than the distance around the rim. Cut each of the two ends of the willow to a needle-sharp point, so that they will overlap neatly. Poke holes all around the rim, and use some spruce root to sew the willow into place with a whip stitch.

## Pottery

It is the Indians of the Southwest who are most famous for their beautiful pottery, although pottery was made to some extent in almost every part of the United States and southern Canada. Pottery is easy to make, if you are lucky enough to have clay in your area. Clay looks like mud, but it acts quite differently. Wet clay feels very much like a bar of soap; the lumps are quite slippery. If you press your finger into clay, you can see your fingerprints very clearly. And if you mold the clay into a long "sausage," you can then tie it in a knot. Ordinary mud isn't like that.

Clay can be almost any color, because it often contains iron or other minerals.

You are most likely to find clay along a riverbank, or down on the bottom of a stream, or along a lakeshore—somewhere where the ground has eroded away. In dry climates, the local clay can be completely dried out, but after a good rain it will be easy to recognize.

If the clay has stones in it, squeeze the clay to expose them and pick them out. When the clay is clean, keep it sitting in the bottom of a bucket of water if you aren't going to use it right away. If the clay has already dried out, it might have to sit in the water for several days.

Pure clay, however, is no good for pottery. It will crack as it is drying. So you have to add some kind of material to prevent this from happening. The material is called tempering, and almost anything will do: hair, plant fiber, clamshells that have been burned and crushed, crushed bits of old pottery, and crushed mica were all used by the Indians. The most common material was sand, but it gives a gritty texture to the finished pot. It's very hard to say how much tempering you should add; some pots had just a tiny bit added, some other pots had more tempering than clay. The more tempering you add, the more easily the pot will break if you drop it, but at the same time it will be less likely to crack when it is heated for cooking. A good proportion to try would be about one handful of tempering to about five handfuls of clay. Mix them together really well.

Some kinds of pots were what we now call thumb pots. They were simply made from a lump of clay that had been hollowed out with the two thumbs. Indian children made pots like this when they were first learning, and adults used this simple method too, if they were making small pots.

But most pots were made by a method called coiling. You start by pressing a lump of clay into a flat round shape for the base of the pot. Actually, that's not quite true; Indian pots in the early days were never flat on the bottom, they were slightly rounded so that they could sit in the ashes or sand in a fireplace. But you might want to make your pot flat-bottomed, so that it will sit on a table.

Take another lump of clay and roll it into a sausage shape. Press this sausage around the rim of the base, coiling the clay around like a snake (Figure 10-10). Keep pressing it all together as you go around, so that the shape of the coil disappears and the pot starts to get a smooth surface. When your first spiral starts to run out, make another and press that into shape like the first. Keep your hands wet all the time, so that the clay won't stick to your fingers. Don't actually drench the pot as you're making it, because if the clay is too soggy, it will sag, and you'll have a puddle rather than a pot.

It's nice to have a pot that is fairly large, and yet which has fairly thin walls. It isn't always easy to make a pot that has walls that are both high and thin, however. The higher the pot gets, the more likely it is to sag. If you're having trouble, let the pot dry out for an hour or so before you continue. That way it will be a little firmer.

In order to get the inner and outer walls smooth, you can use smooth round pebbles to rub the pot, or you can make a little wooden paddle and smack the clay to give it a more uniform finish. But the main thing is that you must have the clay the same thickness all over, from top to bottom, if you really want to be sure that the clay won't crack later on.

When you've finished shaping the pot, let it dry out for several hours, somewhere in the shade. When it's dried to a leathery or rubbery kind of texture, scrape it with a knife or clamshell, or something like that, to get rid of any remaining bumps. Then let the pot dry completely, for several days or weeks. If it isn't bone-dry when you fire it, the pot will crack.

Indian pots were never glazed; they never had the shiny surface that you see on most modern pottery. Sometimes, however, a slightly smoother surface was produced by giving them a coat of slip after they had dried but before they were fired. Slip is just very watery clay, poured over the outside of the pot.

Find a patch of sand or rock to fire your pot. Turn the pot upside down, with a few flat rocks under it to let the heat and air into the inside of the pot, and pile it with tinder and dry twigs. Gently lay some dry split logs over all this. Set it on fire. When you've got a good blaze going, let it burn for about an hour. Add more wood if you start to run out before the end of that hour. Then pull the burning wood aside, gently remove your pot, and let it cool.

There's never any guarantee that a pot won't crack during the firing. If you follow all the above direc-

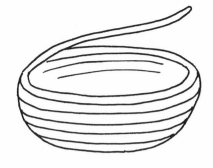

**10-10**
**pottery coiling**

tions, and yet all your pots crack, it might be that the clay you're using is simply no good. But unless that's the case, the odds are that if you make several pots at once, at least one or two will turn out well.

# 11

# BOWS AND ARROWS

Indians hunted with a several different kinds of weapons—spears, slings, bolas, simple throwing sticks, and so on—but most Indians preferred hunting with a bow and arrows. Indian bows were not usually very long: four feet was about the average, and some of the bows of the Plains Indians were only about three feet long. The string could be made out of twisted sinew, or out of rawhide, or it might be made out of plant fiber. The arrow had shafts made out of any sort of straight branches, although cane and reed were often used instead. The arrowheads were made, as we have already seen, out of stone or bone most often, but all sorts of other materials were also available: shell, horn, ivory, even just pieces of hard wood.

If you would like to make an Indian bow, you first have to find a tree with a trunk about four inches thick, and the trunk must be perfectly straight for four or five feet and have no branches or knots—or at least, if there are knots, they should be very small and very tight. But it is also important that you choose the right kind of tree. Some of the best woods are yew, ash, hickory, and oak. Good-sized yew trees are only found on the west coast, but ash, hickory, and oak can be found in most parts of North America. Osage orange was a favorite material on the Plains.

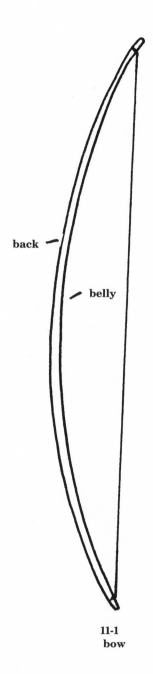

back

belly

11-1
bow

If you can't find one of these types of trees, try to find a small maple, elm, cherry, serviceberry, or willow, although most leafbearing trees (which lumbermen refer to as hardwoods) were used for bows by one Indian group or another. With yew as the one big exception, most needle-bearing trees (the so-called softwoods, although they aren't necessarily softer) are too brittle for making bows. Nevertheless, cedar and juniper were used in some areas, so you might want to try them; I wouldn't recommend pine or spruce.

Chop down the tree and chop or saw the trunk to about four feet in length. Peel off all the bark—a task that is easier in the springtime, when the sap is running. Insert wedges into the small end of the log and split it in half, as I explained in chapter 1. Save the nicest half for the bow.

The side of a bow that is closest to you is called the belly; that's the side you are facing when you're shooting an arrow. The side that is furthest away from you is called the back of the bow. It's important that you know which side of your piece of wood is going to be the back, and which is going to be the belly, or your bow is just going to shatter. The rough side of the wood, the side that was closest to the center of the trunk, is going to be the belly. The smooth side, the side of the wood that had the bark on it, is going to be the back of the bow.

Take a knife or a hatchet and carve away the belly side of the bow to make it a little more rounded. There was a lot of variation in the shape of the belly, so how rounded you make it is up to you. Some bows were almost rectangular in cross section, some were actually quite flat, while others were completely round, like broomsticks. A cross section that is a sort of a rounded rectangle, or perhaps an oval, would be the best sort of shape to aim for. Carve your bow so that it is thicker in the middle, where you'll be holding it to shoot, and narrower toward both tips.

But don't cut away any wood from the back of the bow, the side that had the bark on it. You need the fibers on this side of the bow to remain undamaged. They'll be taking a lot of stress when the bow is bent towards you. In any case, the slightly rounded surface of the back is just about the right shape as it is.

Don't bend the bow very much as you're shaping it. You'll need to bend it occasionally to make sure that it will bend properly when it's finished. But if you bend the bow too much before the bow has dried out, the finished bow might have too much of a curve to it.

It's a bit tricky trying to get both ends of the bow the same shape and thickness. The Indian solution was to finish shaping the bow, not by chopping or slicing it, but by scraping the surface with sharp pieces of broken rock. If you don't have any flint or obsidian, you can use broken glass. Be very careful handling broken glass; it's sharp enough for scraping wood, but it's also sharp enough for you to cut yourself if you're not careful. And make sure you don't leave any glass around for other people to cut themselves on later. Scraping sounds like a slow process, but once you try it you'll be surprised at how quickly it allows you to shape the wood. But if you don't want to try the scraping technique, you can use a modern rasp.

When you've finished shaping the wood, cut a couple of notches at each end, so that you can later fasten on a bowstring. Then get any vegetable or animal oil or fat, and rub the bow thoroughly all over, especially at the ends. This treatment is to make sure that the wood dries slowly and evenly; wood that dries too quickly is likely to form little cracks.

Now put the bow aside for as long as you can, preferably several months. Give it time to season properly. And never leave a bow standing on its end. When a bow isn't actually outside being used, it should lie flat, and the bowstring should always be untied from the top end of the bow.

## The Bowstring

Bowstrings were most often made out of twisted sinew. But rawhide was sometimes used, and for most people these days, rawhide is easier to find than sinew. If the rawhide is dry, soak it until it is flexible, but don't use hot water or you'll weaken the hide. Cut a circular piece about a foot wide. With a

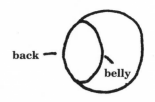

back — belly

**11-2
wood for bow**

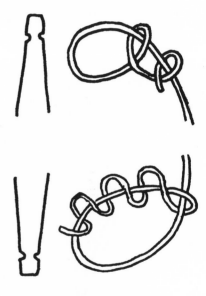

**11-3
knots for bowstring**

pair of scissors, starting on the edge of the circle, cut the rawhide in a spiral, so that you end up with a long strip about a quarter of an inch wide. Keep the rawhide slightly damp, fold it double, and fasten the loop over a small branch or a nail or whatever will hold it firmly in place. Now twist both ends of the thong as tightly as you can get them, and pull on them at the same time to stretch the rawhide. Twist both ends the same way—either clockwise or counterclockwise. After you've twisted an inch or so, turn the two thongs around each other in the opposite direction, as tightly as you can get them. Keep going that way until you've done about four or five feet. Fasten the end with a knot. Let it dry, and you have a fairly stiff but strong bowstring.

Sinew and rawhide both make good string, but they can soften and fall apart fairly rapidly in wet weather. For that reason, Indians sometimes preferred to make string out of plant fiber.

Fasten the string to the bow with the knots shown in the drawings: a timber hitch at the bottom and two half hitches at the top. But keep the bow unstrung when you're not using it.

## Arrows

An arrow consists of three main parts: the shaft, the point, and the feathering.

Shafts were made from the shoots of almost any kind of tree; all that mattered is that they were straight. One of the most popular species was juneberry, which also goes by the names of serviceberry, saskatoon, and shadbush. In the southeastern United States, Indians used cane, a bamboo-like plant with very straight hollow stems. In other areas, people used the equally straight stems of reed, *Phragmites communis*, a tall marsh plant with a top like an ostrich tail (don't confuse it with cattail or rush or other plants that are sometimes inaccurately called reeds).

If you're using the shoots of trees, look for ones that are a bit thicker than a pencil, and trim them so that they're about two feet long. Spring is a good time for this job, because you'll have to peel off the bark.

Collect a good dozen or more shoots, tie them together tightly, and leave the bundle lying on its side for several months. By being tied together that way, they help each other to straighten out.

Leave the rest of the task for winter. Then untie the bundle and take a look at the shafts. If any of them are still crooked, bend them gently with your hands to get rid of the kinks. The task of bending them is made easier by holding them above a fire for a few seconds, but only long enough to warm them, not so long that they start to burn. Then you can make a shaft-scraper by taking one of your stone knives and chipping a small U-shaped notch into its edge; scrape all the shafts with this tool to get rid of any lumps and bumps in the wood. Then get two small pieces of fine sandstone, hold them in one hand, and run the arrow shafts between them to finish the job.

Cut a shallow U-shaped notch in the back end of the shaft, so that it will fit up against the bowstring when you're ready to shoot the arrow. Then take a fine-tipped knife and cut another U-shaped notch at the front end of the shaft. This notch should be fairly wide, because it has to hold the entire thickness of the arrowhead. To get the notch wide enough, twirl the knife tip into the shaft a quarter-inch down from the end, so that you are, in effect, drilling a hole through the shaft. Make sure that this notch for the arrowhead is in line with the notch that holds the bowstring.

Arrows were made with either two or three feathers. For the sake of simplicity, let's talk about how to make an arrow with two feathers. You'll need a donation from a few large birds: crow, duck, goose, or gull feathers are fine. It doesn't matter what kind of feathers you use as long as they're at least six inches long. Look on the ground around a lakeshore or perhaps in a park; birds tend to lose their feathers at particular times of year, so if you hit the molting season you're in luck. Wing feathers were most often used, although tail feathers also work. Wing feathers have a definite left or right curve at the top; tail feathers don't.

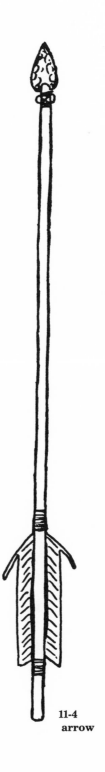

**11-4
arrow**

If you use wing feathers, notice that the feathers have a top side and a bottom side. If you put all your feathers on a table with all the top sides up, you'll see that some of the feathers curve to the left, and some of them curve to the right, depending on whether they came from the left wing of a bird or the right wing. You'll need to select two feathers for each arrow. Make sure that those two feathers have the same curve: you'll need either two rights or two lefts.

Split each feather all along the shaft, and throw away the smaller side of the feather. Chop the ends off the remaining half, so that you have a piece about four or five inches long. Then peel the barbs away from the shaft of the feather, at both ends, so that you've got a little spike at each end, which will then be tied down onto the shaft of the arrow. Finally, slice off the outer edge of the feathering, to make it a bit narrower all along its length.

Take your second feather and make another piece of feathering just like the first one, and then you're ready to tie them both to the wooden shaft. The feathering was normally tied on with sinew, so try to get some thin pieces of sinew, several inches long. Hold the sinew in your mouth for a few seconds to wet it and make it more flexible. If you don't have any sinew, waxed dental floss is a good substitute, although it lacks the natural glue of sinew.

Fastening the feathering onto an arrow can be a bit of a clumsy job, but here's how to make the job easier. Tuck the shaft under your left arm (if you're right handed), with the back end pointing forward, and hold that back end with your left hand. Hold the two pieces of feathering on opposite sides of the shaft and tie them onto the shaft with several turns of sinew or floss.

Finally, it's time to turn the arrow around and fasten on the point, the arrowhead. Fit the arrowhead carefully into the notch, whittling away more wood if necessary. Then tie the head on carefully with several dozen tight turns of sinew or floss. If you've made the arrowhead with a stem, or with two notches, it will fit better than a more rounded type of head. Sometimes warm pitch was spread on as a glue. You can collect pitch from wounds in the bark of any needle-bearing tree; pine or spruce will do, but balsam fir has convenient bubbles on its bark, which can be popped to supply clear pitch. Spread it over the base of the arrowhead, and then hold it over a fire just enough to melt it into a bit smoother form—but not enough to set it on fire.

Or just stick a wad of dried pitch in your mouth and chew it. After a minute it'll lose its strong taste and start looking and feeling like ordinary chewing gum. (In fact, at one time spruce gum was sold in stores as chewing gum—maybe it still is.) Take it out of your mouth and mold it into place between the shaft and the point.

Tie a leather strap onto your left wrist to prevent it from being stung by the bowstring. Then make yourself a quiver by getting a piece of leather about one foot by two feet, folding it in half lengthwise, and sewing it up. Fasten a strap to the top and bottom so that you can hold the quiver on your back. Quivers came in many different shapes and sizes, so it's impossible to describe any correct pattern. The Indians of the Northwest Coast made a long box out of cedar wood, open at one end, while some of the Eskimos even took an entire salmon skin and dried it for use as a quiver.

# ZIGGURAT BOOKS
## FROM CHICAGO REVIEW PRESS

**Ziggurat**   A temple of the ancient Assyrians and Babylonians, having the form of a terraced pyramid of successively receding stories. Assyrian *ziqquratu*, summit, mountain top, from *zaqaru*, to be high.          —*American Heritage Dictionary of the English Language*

**Ziggurat Books** are project books for talented young people of middle and high school age, ten or eleven and up. Many are science or technology oriented; others involve literature or the fine and applied arts. All emphasize a hands-on, experimental approach to adult disciplines such as photography, astronomy, the graphic arts, architecture, fashion, and interior design.

**Ziggurat Books** give students a taste of a wide variety of adult professions. They provide innovative, challenging material for science and art fairs, class and individual school projects. Most important, they enable young people to explore their talents as they experience the effort and the excitement of creative work.

**Ziggurat Books** are published by Chicago Review Press and distributed by Independent Publishers Group. Both offices are located at 814 North Franklin Street, Chicago, Illinois, 60610, (312) 337-0747, (800) 888-4741.